MICROSO

Ou

Field Guide

PUBLISHED BY

Microsoft Press
A Division of Microsoft Corporation
One Microsoft Way
Redmond, Washington 98052-6399

Library of Congress Cataloging-in-Publication Data
Nelson, Stephen L., 1959-
Microsoft Outlook 97 Field guide/Stephen L. Nelson.
p. cm.
Includes index.
ISBN 1-57231-383-8
1. Microsoft Outlook 2. Time management--Computer programs. 3. Personal information management--Computer programs I. Title.
HD69.T54N45 1997
005.369--dc20 96-36635
CIP

Printed and bound in the United States of America.

3 4 5 6 7 8 9QMQM2 1 0 9 8 7

Distributed to the book trade in Canada by Macmillan of Canada, a division of Canada Publishing Corporation.

A CIP catalogue record for this book is available from the British Library.

Microsoft Press books are available through booksellers and distributors worldwide. For further information about international editions, contact your local Microsoft Corporation office. Or contact Microsoft Press International directly at fax (206) 936-7329.

Acquisitions Editor: Susanne Freet

Project Editor: Maureen Williams Zimmerman

Technical Editor: Jean Ross

MICROSOFT®

OUTLOOK™ 97

Field Guide

Stephen L. Nelson

Microsoft Press

The Microsoft Outlook 97 Field Guide *is divided into four sections. These sections are designed to help you find the information you need quickly.*

1 ENVIRONMENT

Terms and ideas you'll want to know to get the most out of Outlook. All the basic parts of Outlook 97 are shown and explained. The emphasis here is on quick answers, but most topics are cross-referenced so you can find out more if you want to.

Diagrams of key windows components, with quick definitions, cross-referenced to more complete information.

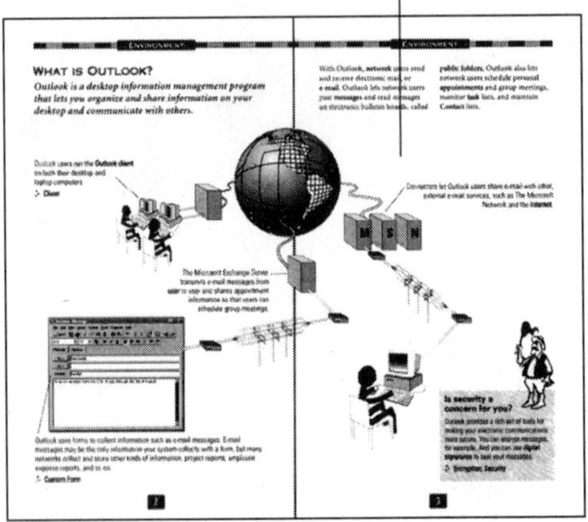

Tipmeister

Watch for me as you use this Field Guide. I'll point out helpful hints and let you know what to watch for.

15 Outlook A to Z

An alphabetic list of commands, tasks, terms, and procedures.

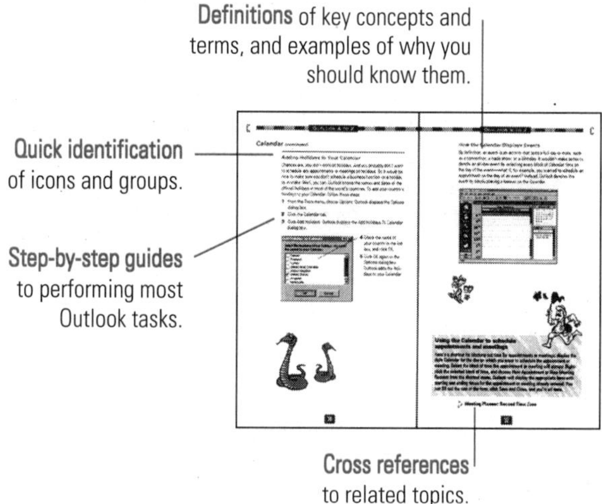

153 Troubleshooting

A guide to common problems—how to avoid them, and what to do when they occur.

163 Quick Reference

Useful indexes, including a full list of menu commands, shortcut keys, and more.

183 Index

A complete reference to all elements of the Field Guide.

INTRODUCTION

In the field and on expedition, you need practical solutions. Fast. This Field Guide provides just these sorts of lightning-quick answers. But take two minutes now and read the introduction. It explains how this unusual little book works.

WHAT IS A FIELD GUIDE?

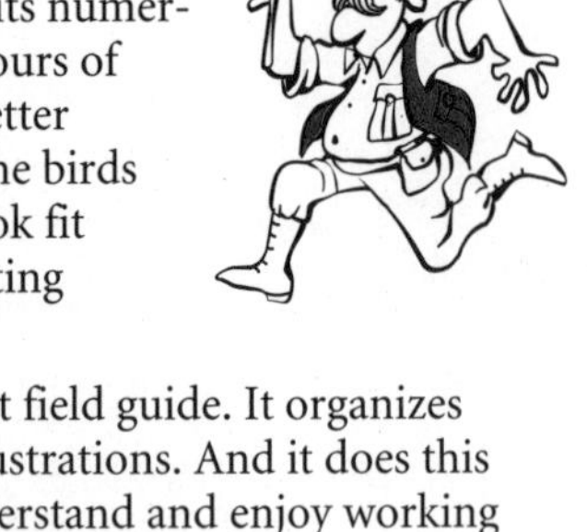

Sometime during grade school, my parents gave me a field guide to North American birds. With its visual approach, its maps, and its numerous illustrations, that guide delivered hours of enjoyment. The book also helped me better understand and more fully appreciate the birds in my neighborhood. And the small book fit neatly in a child's rucksack. But I'm getting off the track.

This book works in the same way as that field guide. It organizes information visually with numerous illustrations. And it does this in a way that helps you more easily understand and enjoy working with Microsoft Outlook 97. For new users, the Field Guide provides the essential information necessary to start using Outlook. But the Field Guide isn't only for beginners. For experienced users, the Field Guide provides concise, easy-to-find descriptions of Outlook tasks, terms, and techniques.

WHEN YOU HAVE A QUESTION

Let me explain then how to find the information you need. You'll usually want to flip first to the Environment section, which is really a visual index. You find the picture that shows what you want to do or the task you have a question about. If you want to know how to send e-mail messages, you flip to pages 4 and 5, which talk about how you send an e-mail message over a network using Outlook.

Next you read the captions that describe the parts of the picture. Say, for example, that you want to send a file along with your message. On page 5, there's a caption that describes what message attachments are.

You'll notice that some captions use boldface terms or are followed by a little paw print and additional **boldface** terms. These refer to entries in the second section, Outlook A to Z, and provide more information related to the caption's contents. (The paw print shows you how to track down the information you need. Get it?)

Outlook A to Z is a dictionary of more than 100 entries that define terms and describe tasks. (After you've worked with Outlook a bit or if you're already an experienced user, you'll often be able to turn directly to this section.) So if you have just read the caption that talks about message attachments, you'll see the term **OLE** object in boldface, indicating a cross-reference. If you don't know what an OLE object is, you can flip to the OLE entry in Outlook A to Z.

When an entry in Outlook A to Z appears as a term within another entry, I'll show it in **boldface** the first time it appears in that entry. For example, as part of describing what OLE is, I might tell you that you use OLE to create a compound document file. In this case, the word **file** appears in bold letters—alerting you to the presence of another entry explaining the term file. If you don't understand the term or want to do a bit of brushing up, you can flip to the entry for more information.

When You Have a Problem

The third section, Troubleshooting, describes problems that new and casual users of Outlook often encounter. Following each problem description, I list one or more solutions you can employ to fix the problem.

When You Wonder about a Command

The Quick Reference at the end of the Field Guide describes the Outlook menu commands and toolbar buttons. If you want to know what a specific command or button does, turn to the Quick Reference. Don't forget about the Index either. You can look there to find all references in this book to any single topic.

CONVENTIONS USED HERE

I have developed two other conventions to make using this book easier for you. Rather than use wordy phrases such as "Activate the File menu and then choose the Print command" to describe how you choose a menu command, I'm just going to say, "Choose Print from the File menu." And rather than say, "Choose the Copy toolbar button from the New Message form toolbar," I'm just going to say, "Click the Copy toolbar button." (I'll show a picture of the toolbar button in the margin.)

One final but important point: when I refer to Windows or Microsoft Windows—unless I specifically say otherwise—I mean either Windows 95 or Windows NT version 4.0.

ENVIRONMENT

Need to get the lay of the land quickly? Then the Environment is the place to start. It defines the key terms you'll need to know and the core ideas you should understand as you begin exploring Microsoft Outlook 97.

WHAT IS OUTLOOK?

Outlook is a desktop information management program that lets you organize and share information on your desktop and communicate with others.

Outlook users run the **Outlook client** on both their desktop and laptop computers.

Client

The Microsoft Exchange Server transmits e-mail messages from **user** to user and shares appointment information so that users can schedule group meetings.

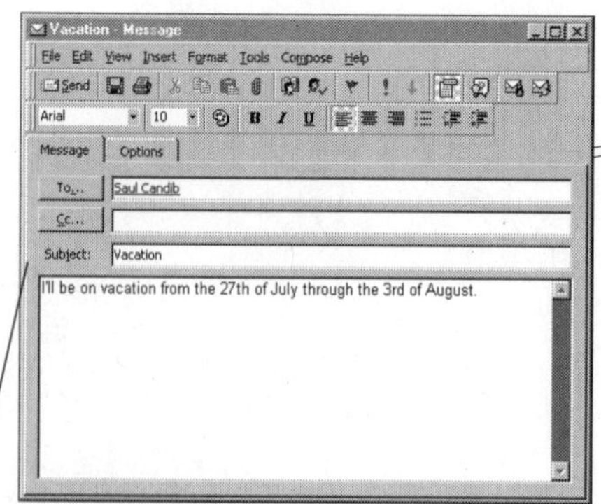

Outlook uses **forms** to collect information such as e-mail messages. E-mail messages may be the only information your system collects with a form, but many networks collect and store other kinds of information: project reports, employee expense reports, and so on.

Custom Form

With Outlook, **network** users send and receive electronic mail, or **e-mail.** Outlook lets network users post **messages** and read messages on electronic bulletin boards, called **public folders.** Outlook also lets network users schedule personal **appointments** and group meetings, monitor **task** lists, and maintain **Contact** lists.

Is security a concern for you?

Outlook provides a rich set of tools for making your electronic communications more secure. You can encrypt messages, for example. And you can use **digital signatures** to seal your messages.

Encryption; Security

SENDING YOUR MESSAGES

With Outlook, network users easily send e-mail messages to other network users and, optionally, over the Internet.

Click the To or Cc button to see the **Address Book.** It lists the names of everyone in your **organization** so you can easily send them messages.

Address Book

Name the **Recipients** of your message by using the To and Cc boxes.

Blind Carbon Copy; Copy; Distribution List; E-Mail Name

The **Message Form** window provides input blanks you use to create your message.

Form

Type the **Message Body** into the main part of the Message form.

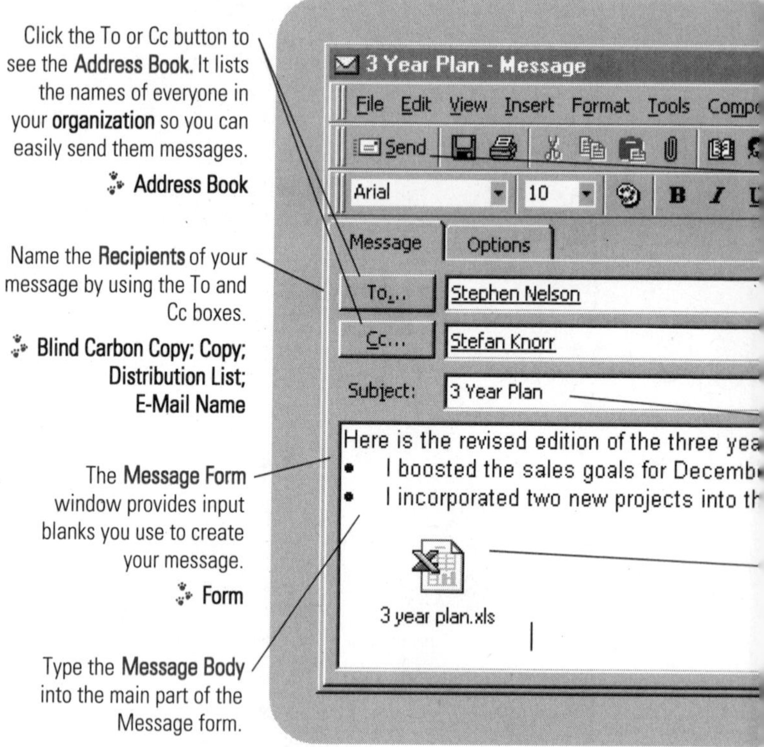

To create an e-mail **message,** you use the **Message form** to name the **recipient,** identify the message **subject,** and then type the body of your message. While text-only e-mail messages are probably most common, you can also use Outlook to e-mail **files** and objects and to **post messages** to electronic bulletin boards, called **public folders,** where anyone can read them.

OLE

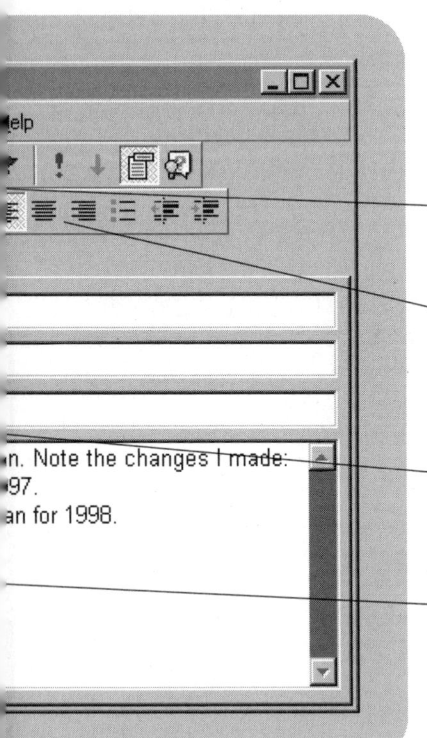

Send your message by clicking the Send button when you finish the message.

Add **Formatting** to your messages by using the **toolbar.**

Alignment; Bullets; Character Formatting; Font

Identify the **message subject** by using the Subject box.

Subject

Message attachments let you send a file, object, or even another message with your message.

Attachment; OLE

READING YOUR MESSAGES

Outlook makes it easy to organize and read your incoming messages. The Inbox is Outlook's message center.

The **Folder List** identifies your personal folders and any of the public folders available for messages. Double-click the Inbox folder to view incoming messages.

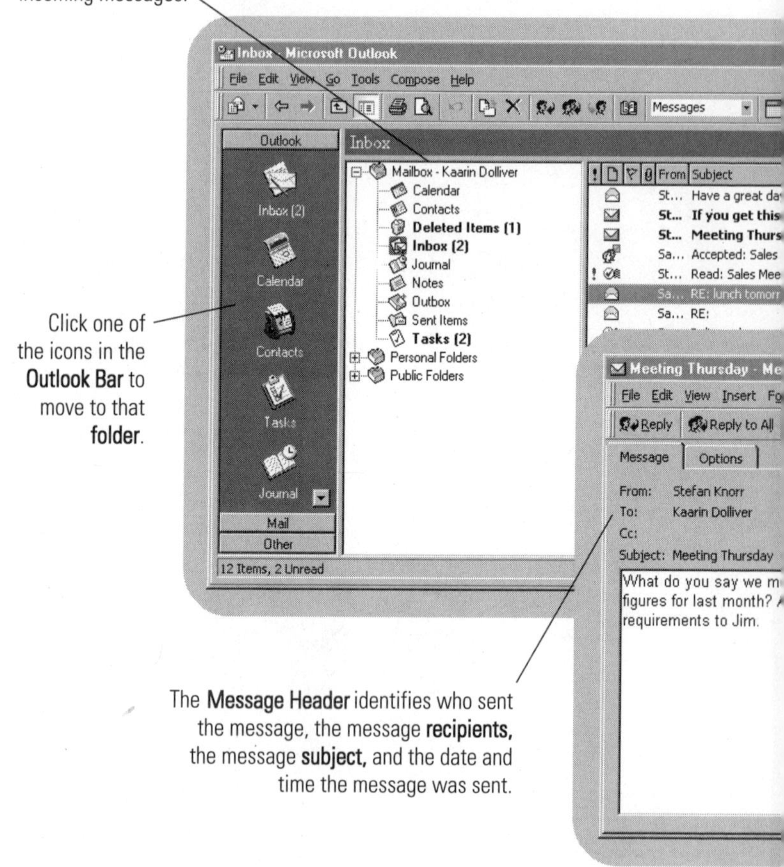

Click one of the icons in the **Outlook Bar** to move to that **folder**.

The **Message Header** identifies who sent the message, the message **recipients,** the message **subject,** and the date and time the message was sent.

Outlook uses **folders** to organize messages. **Private folders** store the messages you receive and copies of messages you send. **Public folders** store **post messages** that senders want to make available to every Outlook **user.** Once you find the folder with the message you want to read, double-click the message to read it.

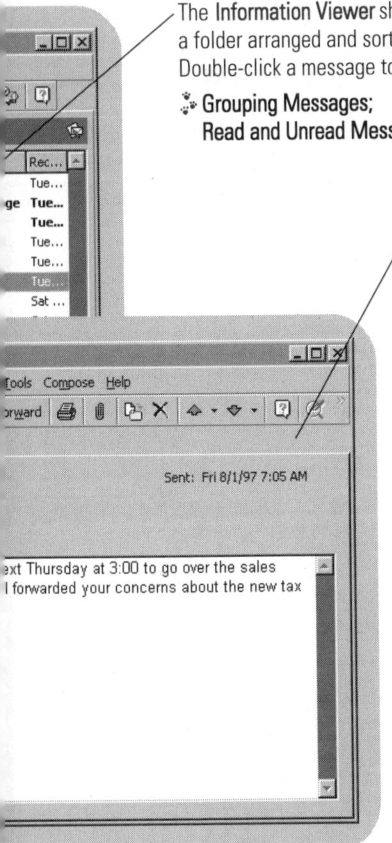

The **Information Viewer** shows the messages in a folder arranged and sorted any way you want. Double-click a message to read it.

Grouping Messages; Read and Unread Messages

A **Message** appears in its own window so you can read it easily. The Message window also provides **toolbar** buttons that you can use to print, delete, **reply** to, or **forward** the message.

Do you need help with your messages?

If you're someone who receives large numbers of messages, Outlook provides two useful tools to help you manage and monitor your incoming messages. The **Rules Wizard** alerts you to messages you receive and also deletes, replies to, or forwards messages. The **Out Of Office Assistant** automatically replies to messages when you're away from your computer.

HOW THE CALENDAR WORKS

Outlook helps you maintain an appointment calendar and a task list.

Click one of the icons in the **Outlook Bar** to move to that **folder**.

Appointments get entered into time-slots in your Calendar.

Appointments; Private Appointments and Tasks; Recurring Appointment

Meetings are easier to schedule because Outlook does the work of finding the earliest open time-slot that the meeting attendees have in common.

Busy Time; Delegate Access Permissions; Meeting Planner;

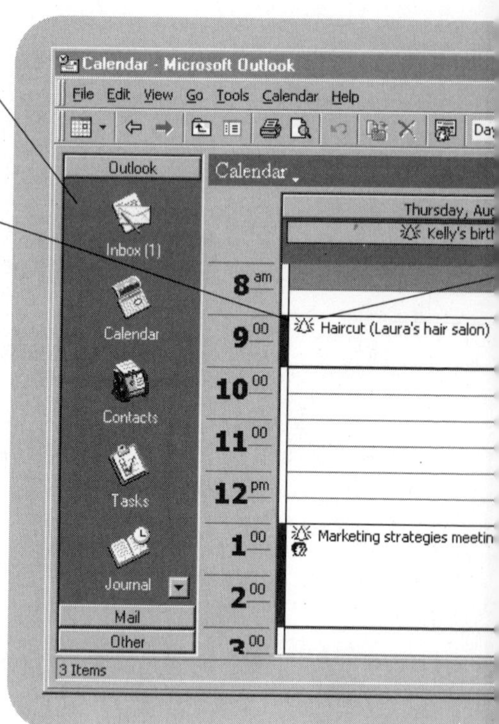

You use the **Calendar** to schedule your time commitments: meetings, **appointments,** deadlines, and so forth. You use the **TaskPad** to keep track of the **tasks** you need to complete.

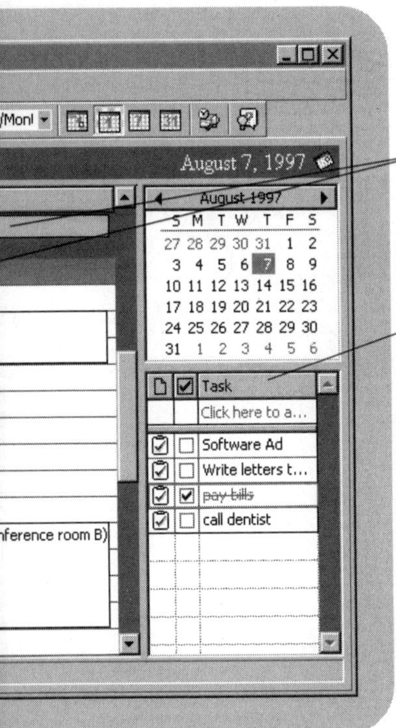

You can tell Outlook to display Reminder Messages that alert you to upcoming appointments and **events.**

The TaskPad is a compact version of the **Task List** that lets you keep track of the individual **tasks** that you need to complete.

Recurring Task

KEEPING TRACK OF YOUR CONTACTS

The Contacts folder lets you keep records of business and personal contacts.

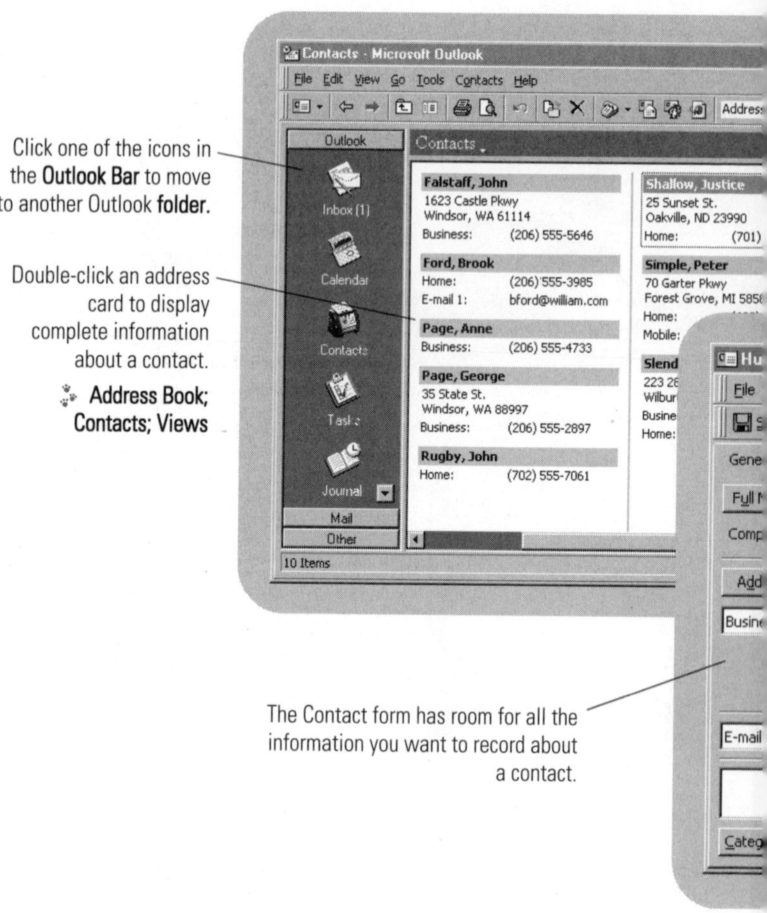

Click one of the icons in the **Outlook Bar** to move to another Outlook **folder**.

Double-click an address card to display complete information about a contact.

Address Book; Contacts; Views

The Contact form has room for all the information you want to record about a contact.

You can use the Contact list to keep track of the names, mailing addresses, phone numbers, and e-mail addresses of all your customers, vendors, contractors, friends, family, and acquaintances. You can display and view information about your contacts in a list or as alphabetized index cards.

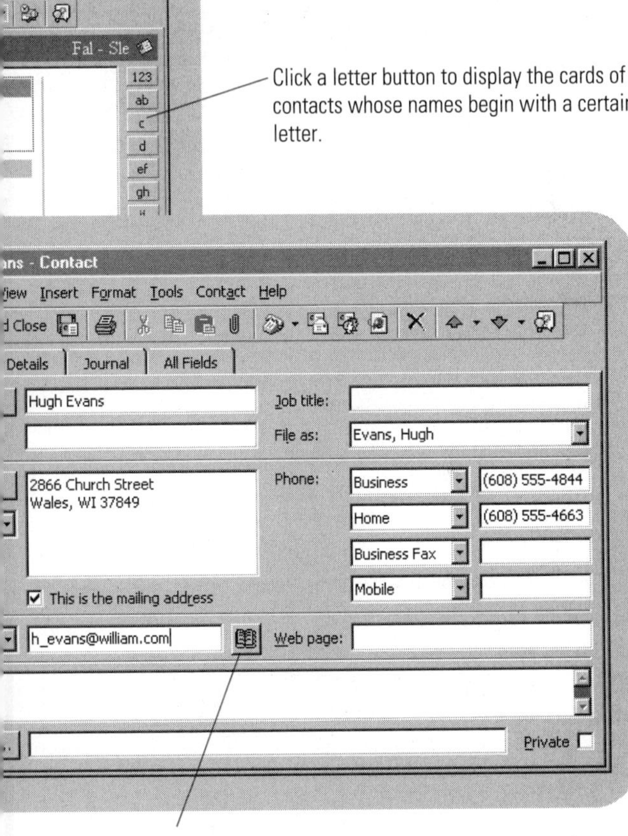

Click a letter button to display the cards of contacts whose names begin with a certain letter.

Click this button to explore the **Web page** of one of your contacts.

World Wide Web

KEEPING A JOURNAL AND WRITING NOTES

The Journal folder lets you track messages, tasks, and even Office files. Notes are handy ways to post reminders.

Click one of the icons in the **Outlook Bar** to move to that **folder**.

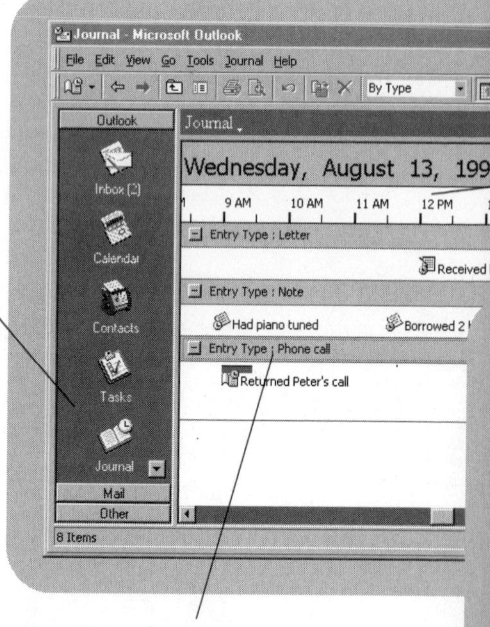

You can group **Journal items** into **categories** to make them easier to find.

You can paste **Notes** just about anywhere, including into **e-mail messages.**

Notes show the date and time they were written.

Use the **Journal** to automatically maintain a running list of all the messages you send and receive, notes you write, tasks you work on, and **Microsoft Word,** Microsoft Excel, and Microsoft PowerPoint files you create. View Journal events against a timeline or in a list. Create sticky notes to paste on your desktop or in messages. Color-code them for easy filing.

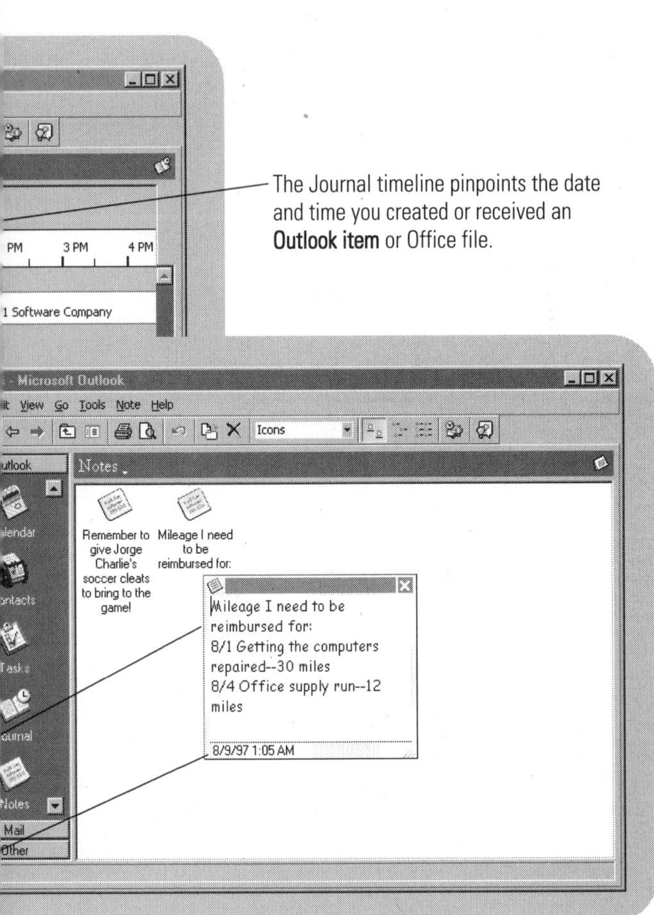

The Journal timeline pinpoints the date and time you created or received an **Outlook item** or Office file.

Change the size and color of notes or minimize them to the Taskbar.

Outlook A to Z

Maybe it's not a jungle out there. But you'll still want to keep a survival kit close at hand. Outlook A to Z, which starts on the next page, is just such a survival kit. It lists in alphabetic order the tools, terms, and techniques you'll need to know.

Actions

Actions Actions are automatic responses you tell Microsoft Outlook to perform in certain situations. For example, you can tell Outlook to open the next **message** on the **Inbox** message list when you close the previous message. You can set controls for most actions on the various tabs of the Options dialog box, which you open by choosing Options from the Tools menu.

Rules Wizard

Address Book

Address Book Because you correspond with other people, you need a convenient place to store their **e-mail names,** telephone numbers, and addresses. Outlook provides one such storage tool in the form of the Address Book. Using the Address Book, you can keep a list of the people with whom you regularly correspond.

Adding E-Mail Names to Your Address Book

Adding the name of someone from whom you've received a **message** is easy. To add the name of such a person to your Address Book, just display the message and then right-click the name of the sender. When Outlook displays the shortcut menu, click Add To Personal Address Book.

Adding an e-mail name to your Address Book when you haven't received a message from the other person requires a bit more work. Click the Address Book button on the Standard toolbar so that Outlook displays the Address Book dialog box. This dialog box lists the names you've already added to your Address Book.

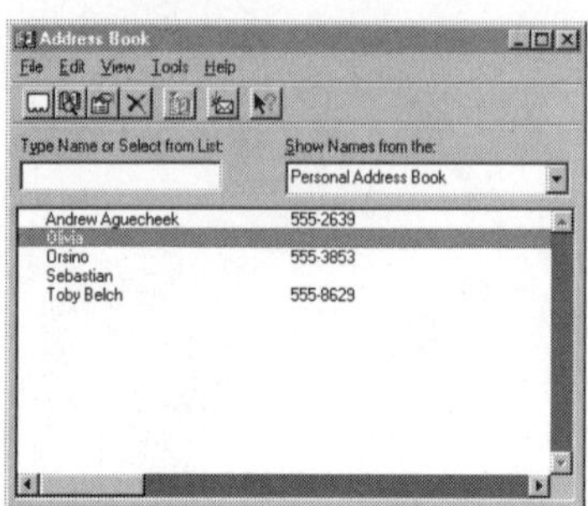

To add a name, click the New Entry toolbar button. When Outlook displays the New Entry dialog box, use it to describe the type of e-mail name you're adding to the Address Book. If you're adding an Internet e-mail name, for example, click Internet Address. If you're adding a Microsoft Network e-mail name, click Microsoft Mail Address. If you want to add a Microsoft Fax name and telephone number, click Microsoft Fax.

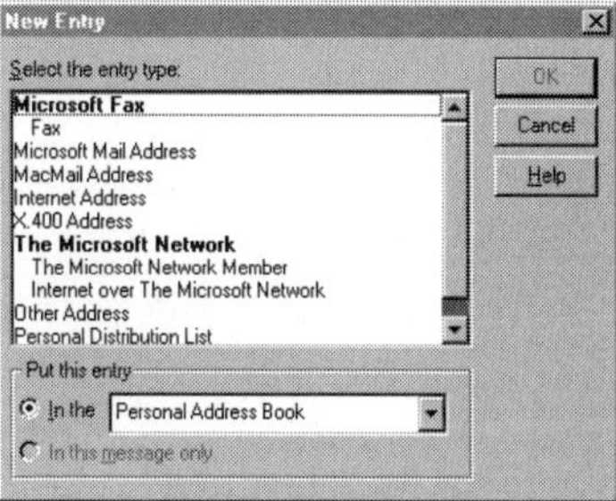

After you identify the type of entry you're adding to the Address Book and click OK, Outlook displays a dialog box that prompts you for the information it needs to actually send the person a message. In the case of an Internet Address entry, for example, you probably want to supply the person's real name, and you definitely need to provide the actual Internet mail address.

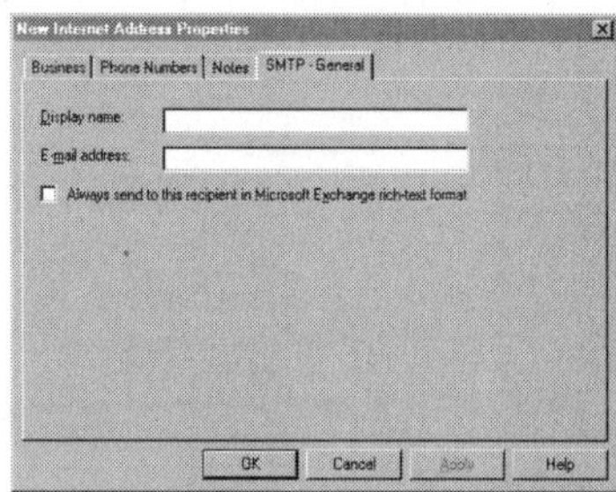

continues

Address Book *(continued)*

Storing Telephone Numbers, Addresses, and Other Information

The Address Book doesn't just store names and e-mail names. You can use it to store company names, street addresses, telephone numbers, fax numbers, and even recent contact information. In effect, you can use the Address Book as an online Rolodex. (And, you can use Outlook's **Contact list** in the same manner.) To record information about someone at the same time that you add an e-mail name to the Address Book, click the Business, Phone Numbers, and Notes tabs and record data there after you record the e-mail name information.

Recording information about someone is easy, even if you're not working with the Address Book. To record the information, click the Address Book button, right-click the name of the person about whom you want to record more information, and click Properties.

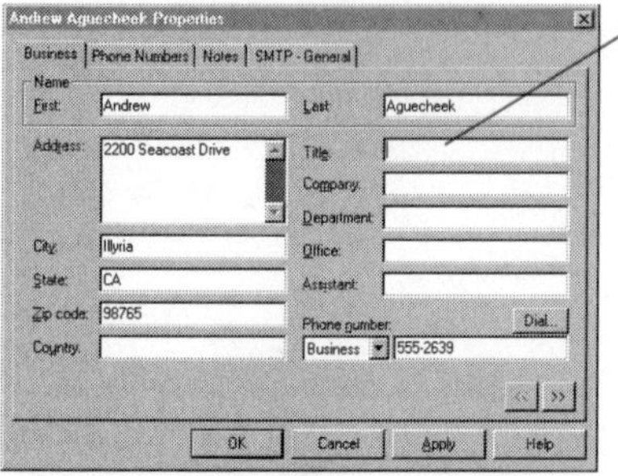

You don't need my help to figure out what goes into these text boxes, right?

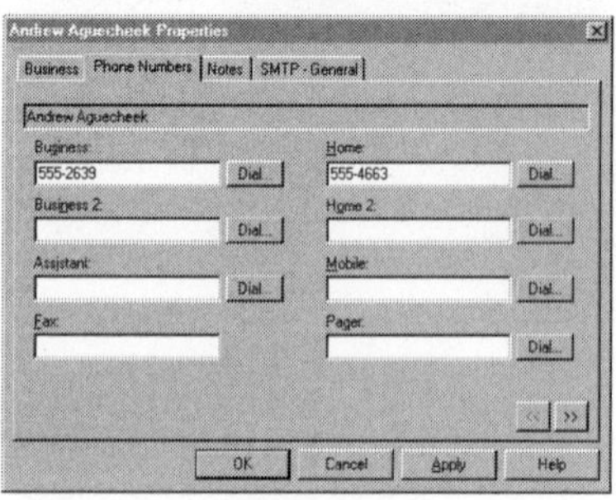

If your modem is connected to the same line as your telephone, you can click one of the Dial buttons to tell Outlook to dial the telephone number stored in the adjacent box. After Outlook dials the number, it displays a message box that tells you to pick up the phone.

Using Address Book Names to Send E-Mail

Typically, you use the information in the Address Book to e-mail someone a message. To do this, click the To or Cc buttons, which appear on the New Message form. When you do, Outlook displays the Select Names dialog box.

Use the Show Names From The list box to specify whether you want to see the names of people on the **Global Address List** or in your **Personal Address Book.** To select someone from the Address Book, double-click a name to add it to the Message Recipients list.

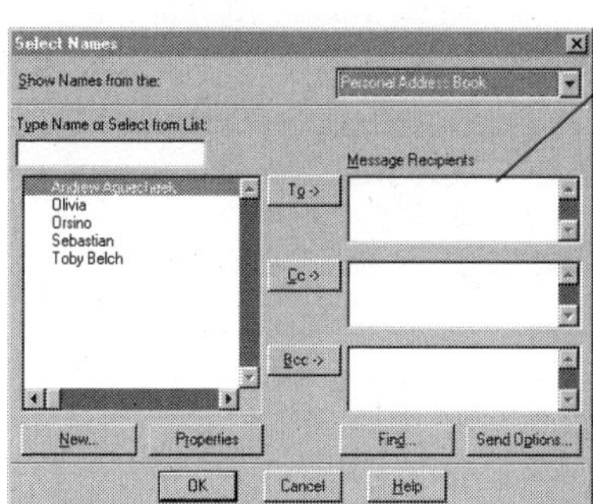

After the names of everyone who should receive the message have been added to the Message Recipients list, click OK.

Contacts

Administrator If you are connected to a network, your administrator is the person whose job it is to take care of the network. This person is probably the same one who told you about Outlook and set up your **mailbox**. You should try to learn who the network administrator is if you don't already know. If you have problems sending a **message** to someone else, you can probably get help from the administrator.

Alignment You can change the alignment of a paragraph or paragraphs in the New Message form. To do this, select the paragraph you want to align by triple-clicking it or select several paragraphs by clicking in one and dragging over the others. Then click the Align Left, Center, or Align Right toolbar buttons.

Annual Event You can add annual events to your calendar. These are simply **events** that occur once a year. Birthdays. Wedding anniversaries. The opening day of fishing season. To add an annual event to your calendar, click Calendar. On the Calendar menu, click New Event. Then use the Event dialog box to describe the event and its timing.

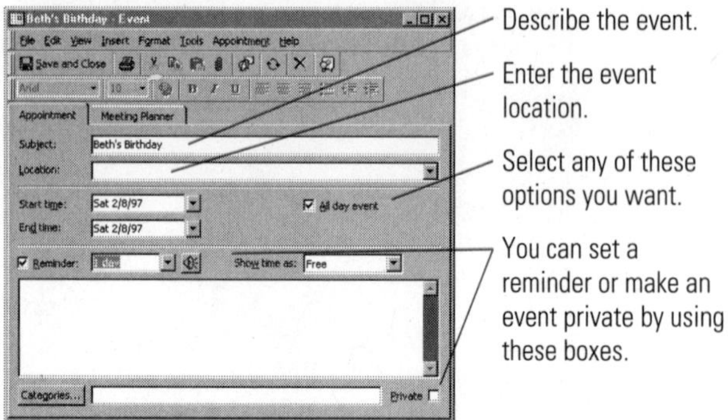

If you're describing a birthday, be sure to allow time for gift shopping. To tell Outlook this is an annual event, click Recurrence on the Appointment menu.

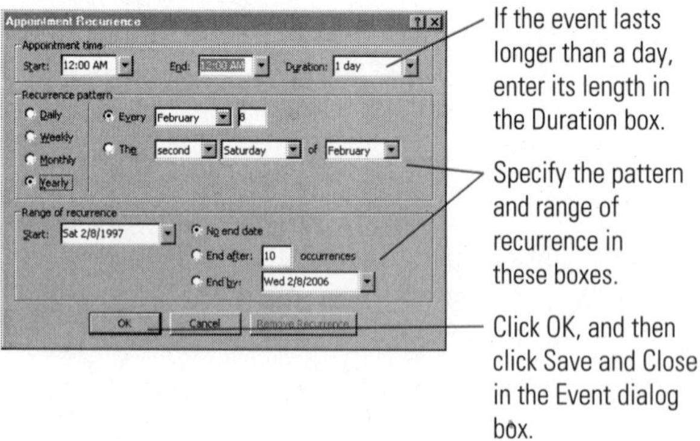

Recurring Appointment; Recurring Task

Appointment Outlook lets you record appointments in the **Calendar**. To add an appointment, click the Calendar icon in the **Outlook Bar**. Click the appointment date on the **Date Navigator**.

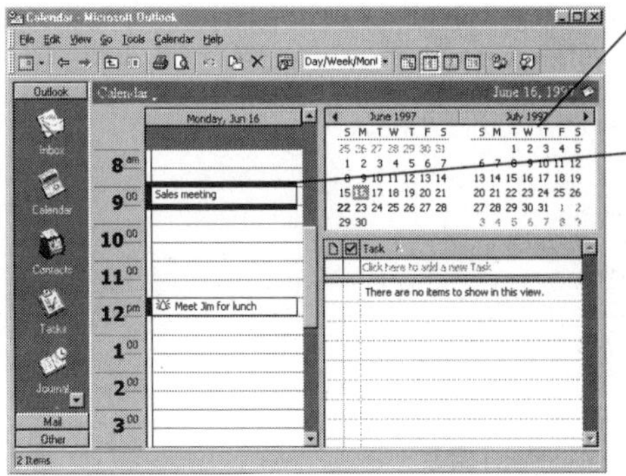

Pick an appointment date here.

Select a time slot, and then type a short description of the appointment.

Alternatively, to provide more detailed information about an appointment you're adding, just double-click any block of time. Or choose New on the File menu, and then click Appointment. Then use the Appointment dialog box to describe the appointment in detail.

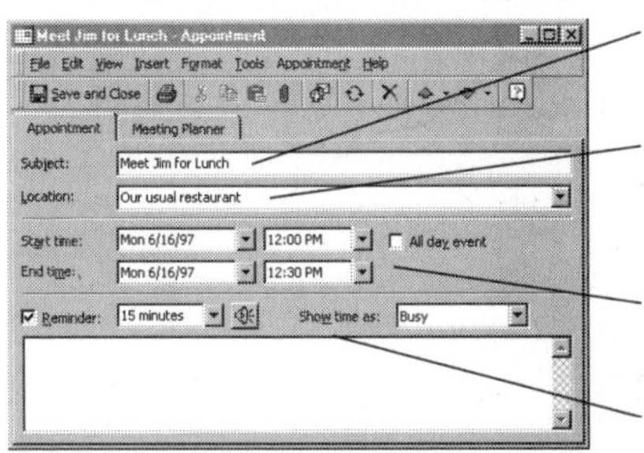

Briefly describe the appointment.

Enter where the appointment will take place.

Enter the start and end times.

Use these boxes to set a reminder, make the appointment private, and describe the appointment in more detail.

Recurring Appointment

Archive Outlook allows you to create archives. An archive is a portion of an existing **Outlook folder** that is stored in a separate file, which is called an archive. For example, suppose you had two years' worth of scheduling information, for 1996 and 1997, in an existing file. You could create an archive for the 1996 scheduling information. This way, the information will no longer appear in your regular schedule—so Outlook will run faster—although the information remains available in the archive in case you ever need it.

Outlook will automatically archive files in the **Inbox, Calendar, Journal,** and Sent Mail folders. What's more, you can tell Outlook to AutoArchive items in other Outlook folders or you can turn off AutoArchive altogether. (You can't archive items in the **Contacts** folder because usually contact items don't become obsolete just because they're old.) And you can tell AutoArchive to delete old items instead of archiving them. To turn on AutoArchive, you first must enable it, and then you must set AutoArchive options for each folder you want to archive.

Enabling AutoArchive

To enable AutoArchive, choose Options from the Tools menu and then click the AutoArchive tab of the Options dialog box.

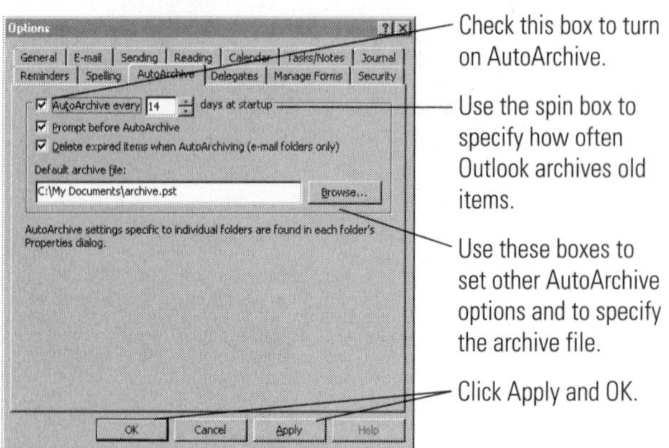

Setting AutoArchive Folder Options

You set AutoArchive options individually for each folder you want to archive. To set options for the **Tasks** folder, for example, right-click the Tasks icon in the **Outlook Bar** and then choose Properties from the **shortcut menu** to display the Tasks Properties dialog box. Click the AutoArchive tab.

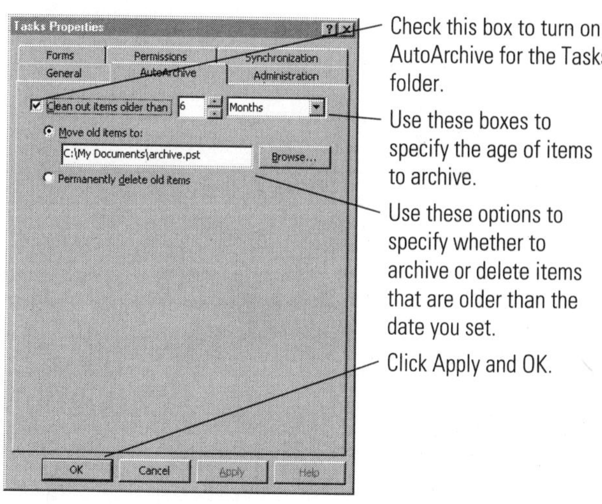

Creating Archives Manually

You can create Outlook archives by choosing Archive from the File menu. In the Archive dialog box, name the archive file, indicate the folder it's currently filed in, and specify the cutoff date.

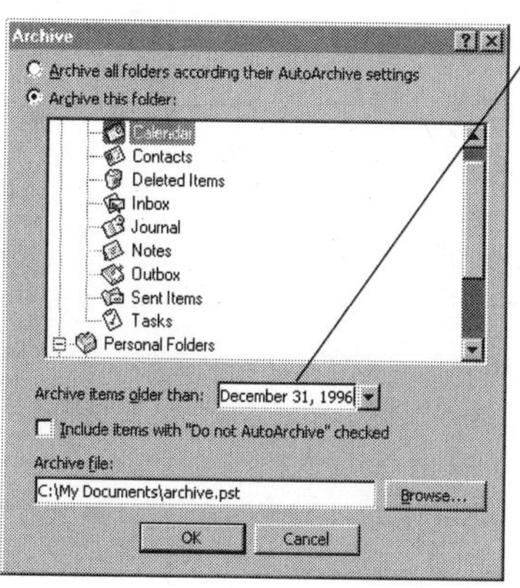

continues

Archive *(continued)*

Retrieving Archives

You retrieve an archive file by adding it to your mailbox. Then you can open it like any other folder in your mailbox. You add the archive file to your mailbox by adding another set of personal folders to your Outlook information service profile. To add another set of personal folders to your profile, choose Services from the Tools menu. Outlook displays the Services dialog box. Click Add. Outlook displays the Add Service To Profile dialog box. Click Personal Folders, and click OK. Outlook displays the Create/Open Personal Folders File dialog box

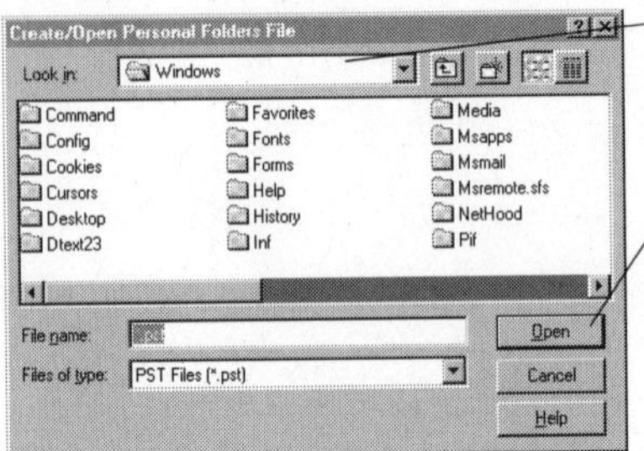

Use the Look In box to identify the archive's location.

Click the archive file, and click Open.

Click OK in the Personal Folders dialog box. Then click OK again in the Services dialog box to add the new folder to your information service profile.

Attachment

Usually when you send a **message,** you simply send something you typed. Perhaps a few kind words. Or maybe a carefully worded warning or criticism. You should know, however, that you can also mail **files,** other messages, and **OLE** objects. To do this, you attach the file, other message, or OLE object to the message you are sending. For help doing this, refer to the Message and **Post Message** entries in this book.

MIME; Uuencode

AutoArchive ❧ Archive

AutoAssistants Outlook comes with a couple of handy tools for managing the **messages** you receive. The **Inbox Assistant** looks at the messages that have arrived in your **Inbox** and then does stuff like alert you to important or interesting messages, delete messages it knows you don't want to read, respond to messages with a standard **reply**, or **forward** messages to other people. The **Out Of Office Assistant** responds to incoming messages when you can't because you're not in the office.

❧ **AutoReply**

AutoDial If you have a modem, and a phone on the same line as the modem, Outlook will make telephone calls for you. In the **Contacts** folder, click AutoDialer on the toolbar. When you click AutoDialer, Outlook displays the New Call dialog box for the selected contact.

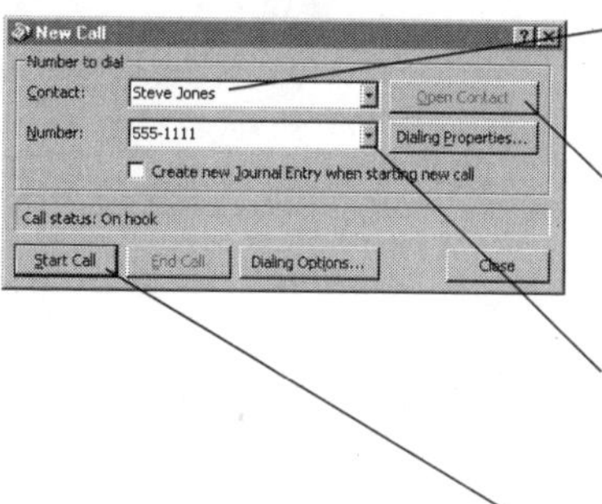

Outlook displays the name of the selected contact here.

Click Open Contact to display the Contact dialog box for the selected contact.

Click here to display all the phone numbers you've recorded for this contact.

Click here to initiate the call.

❧ **Speed Dial**

Automatic Delivery When you click the Send button in the **Message form,** the Outlook **client** immediately sends the **message** to the Microsoft Exchange **server.** Shortly thereafter, the Exchange server sends the message to the recipient's Outlook client. Depending on how the **administrator** set up the server and the client, sending messages can take a few seconds or a few minutes. If your messages aren't being delivered quickly, something is amiss. You need to have a little chat with the administrator.

AutoPreview You can preview the first few lines of all the messages in your **Inbox** information viewer without actually displaying the messages themselves—by clicking the AutoPreview toolbar button or choosing AutoPreview from the View menu.

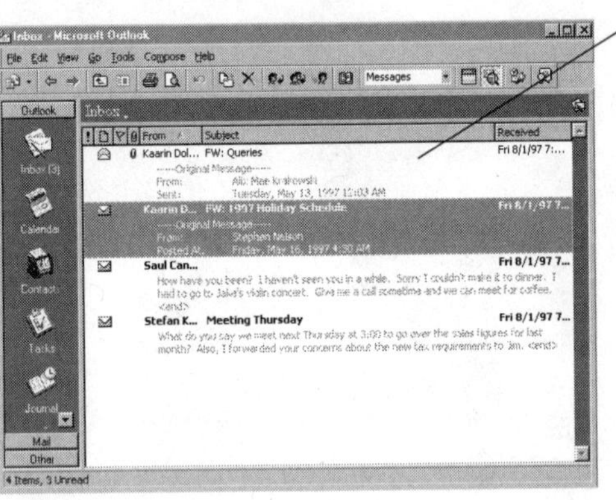

Messages appear like this when AutoPreview mode is turned on.

You can AutoPreview **tasks** in your Task List, too.

AutoReply If you receive office **e-mail,** you can reply automatically to each e-mail message you receive. Automatic replies are especially handy when you want people to know that you can't reply right away because you're on vacation, traveling on business, or simply too busy to respond. To turn on AutoReply, choose **Out Of Office Assistant** from the Tools menu to display the Out Of Office Assistant dialog box.

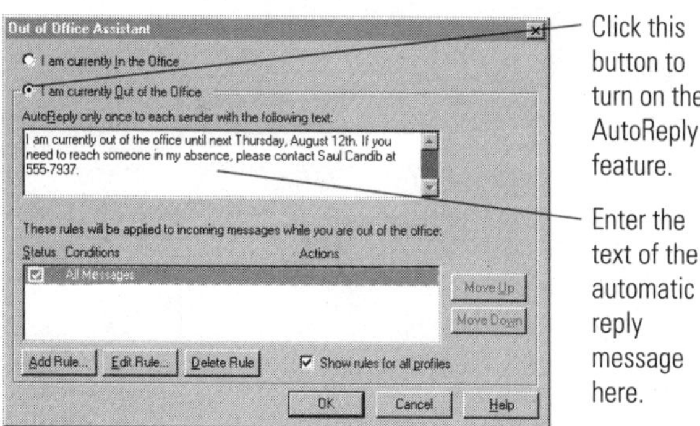

AutoSignature For years now, people—particularly Internet **users**—have been appending little snippets of text called signatures to the ends of their **e-mail messages.** Sometimes signatures list the sender's name, address, and telephone number. But they also include quotations, goofy character-based art, and even randomly generated messages. You can tell Outlook to add a signature to the end of your e-mail messages.

continues

AutoSignature *(continued)*

Creating an AutoSignature

To create an autosignature, click AutoSignature on the Tools menu. When Outlook displays the AutoSignature dialog box, use it to create and format the signature. Then click OK.

Click this box to append the autosignature to all your new messages.

Use the Font and Paragraph buttons to add fancy formatting to your signature.

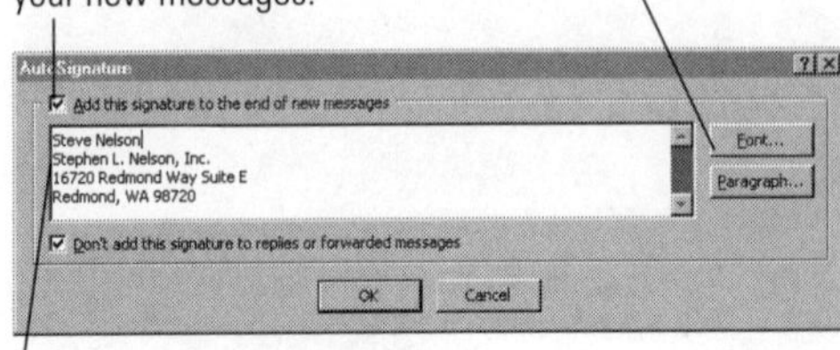

Enter the signature here.

Using AutoSignature

After you create an autosignature and tell Outlook to use it, the autosignature is appended automatically to the end of each of your messages.

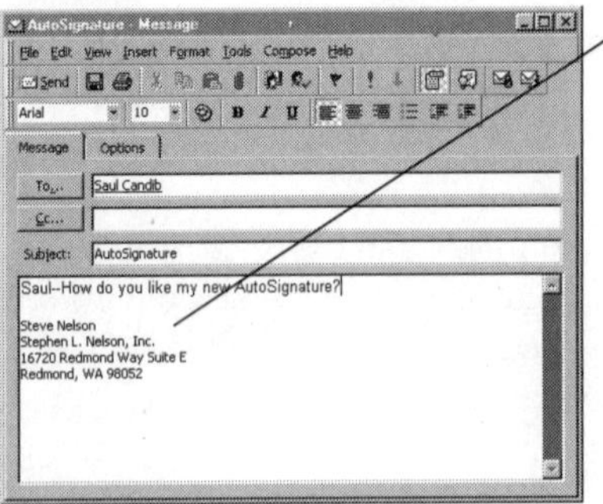

This block of text is the autosignature.

Bcc *See* Blind Carbon Copy

Blind Carbon Copy A blind carbon copy is a **copy** of a **message** sent to one party without the other message **recipients** knowing that the party is getting a copy. For example, a blind carbon copy of an employee's annual review might be sent to the human resources manager of a company without the employee knowing. To send blind carbon copies, choose Bcc Field from the View menu of the **Message form,** and the Bcc box will be displayed. Use the Bcc box to name the recipients to whom you want to send a blind carbon copy of a message.

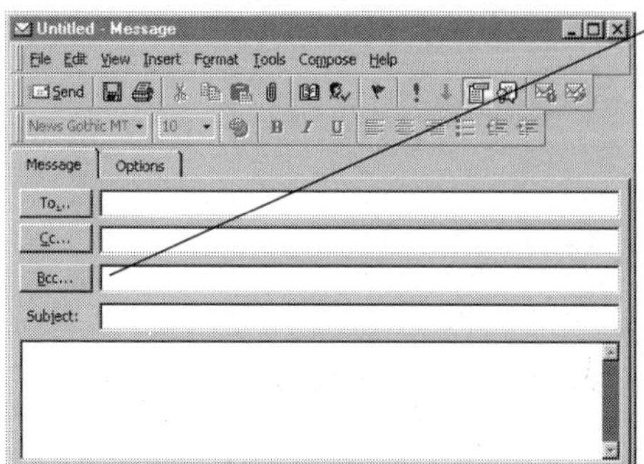

Once you choose Bcc field from the View menu, Outlook adds the Bcc box to the Message form.

Body ❖ **Message Body**

Bullets

Outlook's text editor lets you include bullets in e-mail messages. To do this, select the paragraphs that you want to turn into a bulleted list and click the Bullets toolbar button.

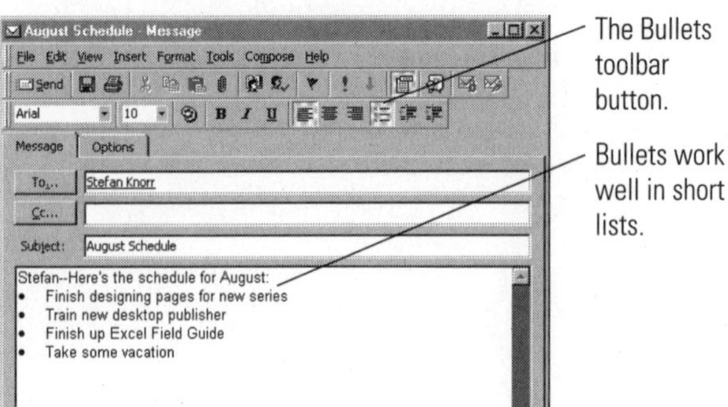

The Bullets toolbar button.

Bullets work well in short lists.

Bullets are a paragraph formatting option

When you click the Bullets tool, Outlook doesn't add a bullet to the beginning of each line but to the beginning of each paragraph you selected. To start each line with a bullet, you need to create short, one-line paragraphs by pressing Enter at the end of each line.

Busy Time Outlook calls the time slots that you've already filled with **appointments** your *busy times*. You can see your busy times blocked out on the **Calendar**. The opposite of busy time is free time, by the way. When you use the **Meeting Planner** to schedule a meeting, the planner looks for free time that the meeting attendees all have in common.

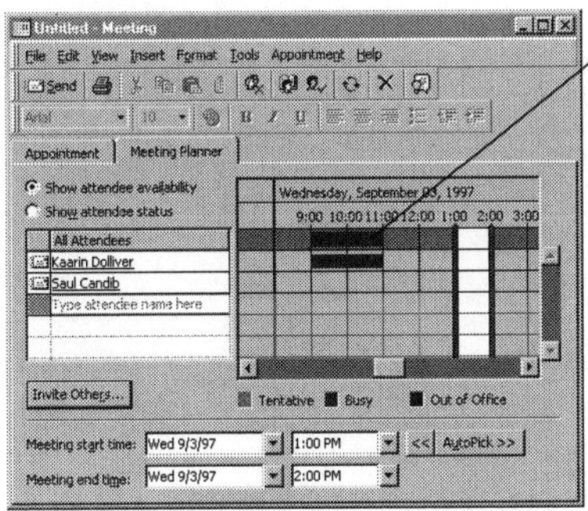

On a color monitor, the busy times appear in blue.

Calendar Calendar is an **Outlook Folder** that lets you schedule **appointments,** meetings, or any of the ordinary activities and **events** that seem to fill up everyone's days. Your dentist appointment. The kids' birthdays. Your anniversary. You get the idea.

If you've used **Schedule+,** Calendar will look pretty familiar to you. (Incidentally, if you're a former Schedule+ user, you can import your old schedule into Outlook. See the entry on the **Import And Export** command.)

continues

Calendar *(continued)*

The Calendar folder has several components.

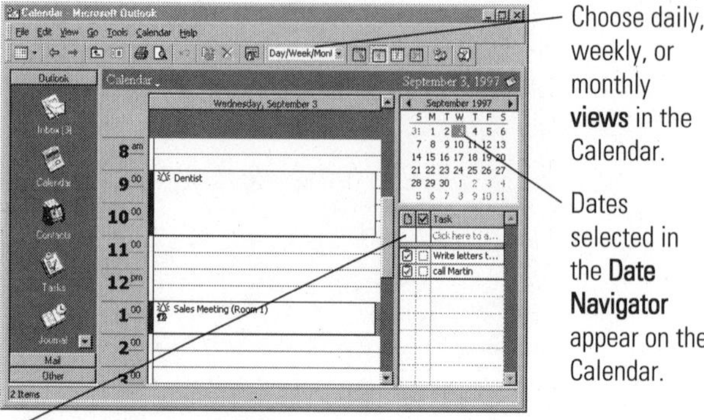

Choose daily, weekly, or monthly **views** in the Calendar.

Dates selected in the **Date Navigator** appear on the Calendar.

Drag a task from the **TaskPad** onto the Calendar to schedule time to work on that task.

Changing the Calendar View

There are so many different ways you can view the Calendar that I can't show them all to you here. So I'll mention just a few. You can experiment with the Calendar on your own to find the views that work best for you.

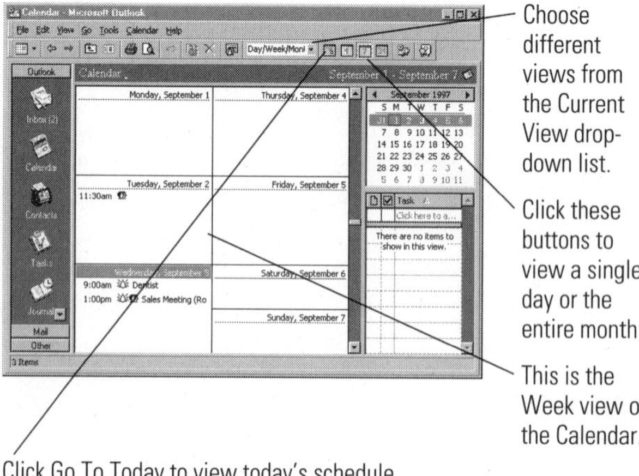

Choose different views from the Current View drop-down list.

Click these buttons to view a single day or the entire month.

This is the Week view of the Calendar.

Click Go To Today to view today's schedule.

Use the Date Navigator to move around in the Calendar.

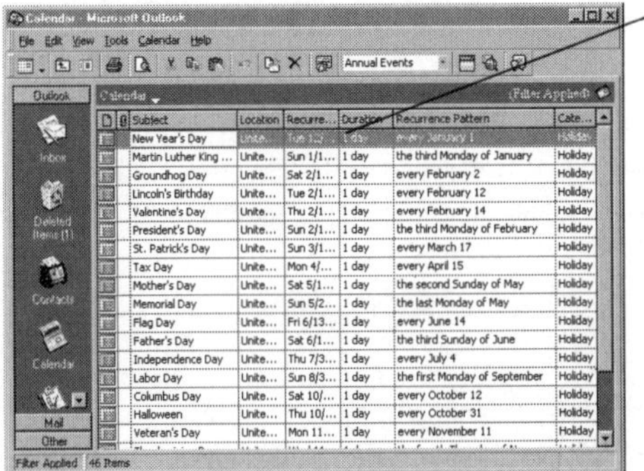

This view shows a list of Annual Events in table form.

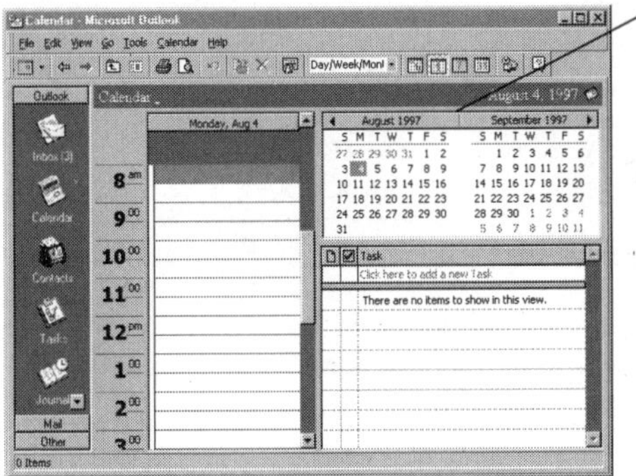

Drag the divider between the Date Navigator and the Calendar to display two months of the Date Navigator simultaneously.

continues

Calendar *(continued)*

Setting Calendar Display Options

On the Calendar tab of the Options dialog box, you can set various Calendar display options, including establishing the work week and designating working hours. To display the Options dialog box, choose Options from the Tools menu. Then click the Calendar tab, and choose the options you want.

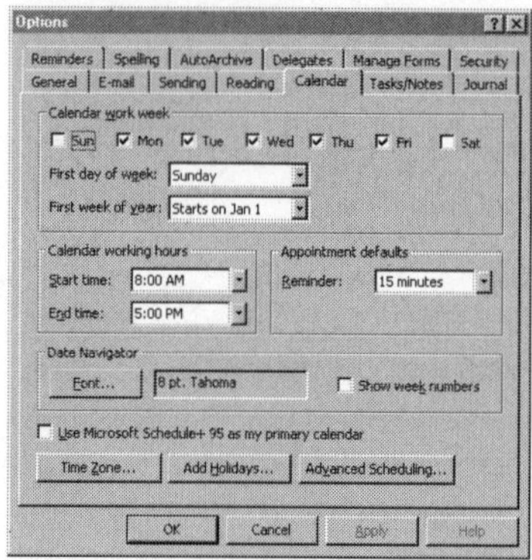

Adding Birthdays and Anniversaries to Your Calendar

Wouldn't it be great to always be reminded of the birthdays of your relatives and friends—*before* they occur? Not to mention your anniversary. You can use Outlook's Calendar to ensure that you'll never again be castigated for your forgetfulness.

Birthdays and anniversaries fall under the category of recurring events. Here's how to enter them into your Calendar:

1 Click the Calendar icon on the Outlook Bar.

2 Choose New Recurring Event from the Calendar menu. Outlook displays the Appointment Recurrence dialog box.

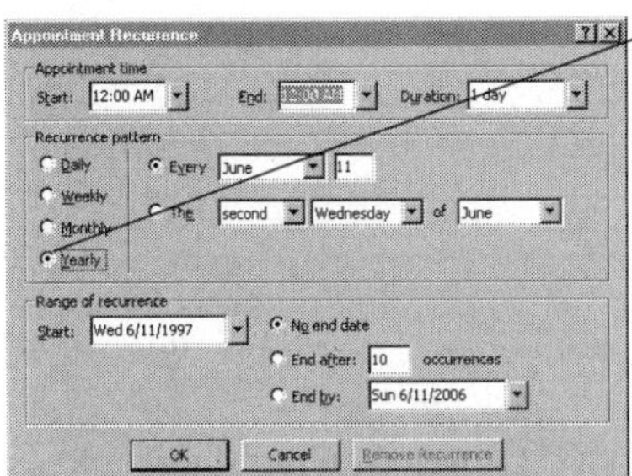

3 Under Recurrence Pattern, click Yearly and enter the date of the birthday or anniversary. Click OK. Outlook displays the Untitled—Event form.

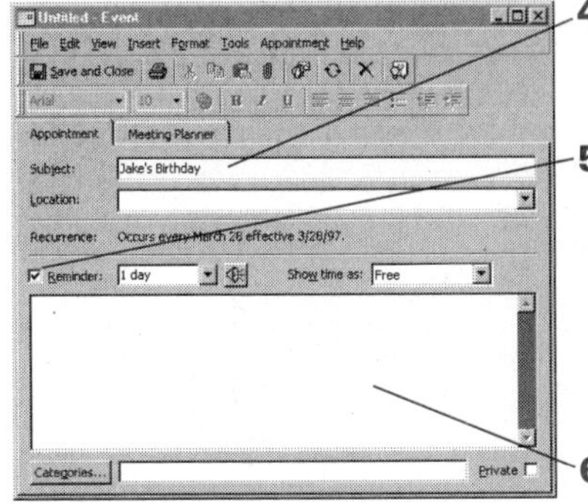

4 In the Subject box, name the birthday or anniversary.

5 Set yourself a reminder—I suggest at least a day or two in advance—longer if you want to send a card or purchase a gift.

6 Type any notes or comments here.

7 Click the Categories button. Outlook displays the Categories dialog box.

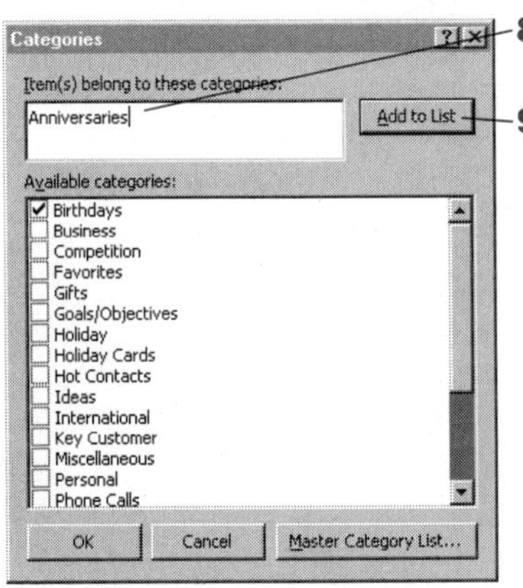

8 Type Birthdays or Anniversaries here.

9 Click Add To List, and then click OK.

Outlook has retitled the Event dialog box with the name of the birthday or anniversary. Click Save and Close.

continues

Calendar *(continued)*

Adding Holidays to Your Calendar

Chances are, you don't work on holidays. And you probably don't want to schedule any appointments or meetings on holidays. So it would be nice to make sure you don't schedule a business function on a holiday by mistake. Well, you can. Outlook knows the names and dates of the official holidays in most of the world's countries. To add your country's holidays to your Calendar, follow these steps:

1. From the Tools menu, choose Options. Outlook displays the Options dialog box.
2. Click the Calendar tab.
3. Click Add Holidays. Outlook displays the Add Holidays To Calendar dialog box.

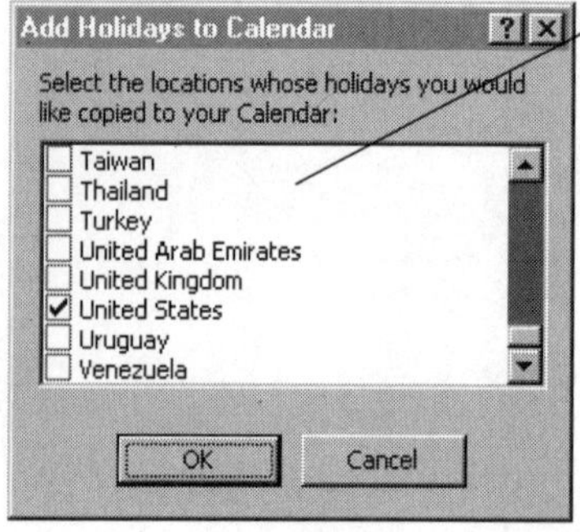

4. Check the name of your country in the list box, and click OK.
5. Click OK again in the Options dialog box. Outlook adds the holidays to your Calendar.

How the Calendar Displays Events

By definition, an event is an activity that lasts a full day or more, such as a convention, a trade show, or a birthday. It wouldn't make sense to denote an all-day event by selecting every block of Calendar time on the day of the event—what if, for example, you wanted to schedule an appointment on the day of an event? Instead, Outlook denotes the event by simply placing a notice on the Calendar.

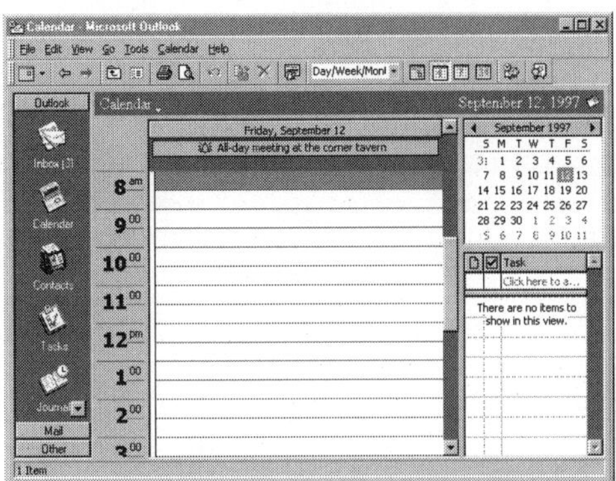

Using the Calendar to schedule appointments and meetings

Here's a shortcut for blocking out time for appointments or meetings: display the daily Calendar for the day on which you want to schedule the appointment or meeting. Select the block of time the appointment or meeting will occupy. Right-click the selected block of time, and choose New Appointment or New Meeting Request from the shortcut menu. Outlook will display the appropriate form with starting and ending times for the appointment or meeting already entered. You just fill out the rest of the form, click Save and Close, and you're all done.

Meeting Planner; Second Time Zone

Categories You can assign Outlook **items** to one of various categories to make them easier to **sort, group,** and **find.** Outlook has 20 built-in categories, including business, personal, ideas, and miscellaneous. And it's easy to create new categories as you need them.

Assigning a Message to a Category

To assign a message to a category, follow these steps:

1. Double-click a message in your Inbox information viewer to display the Message form.
2. Choose Categories from the Edit menu. Outlook displays the Categories dialog box.

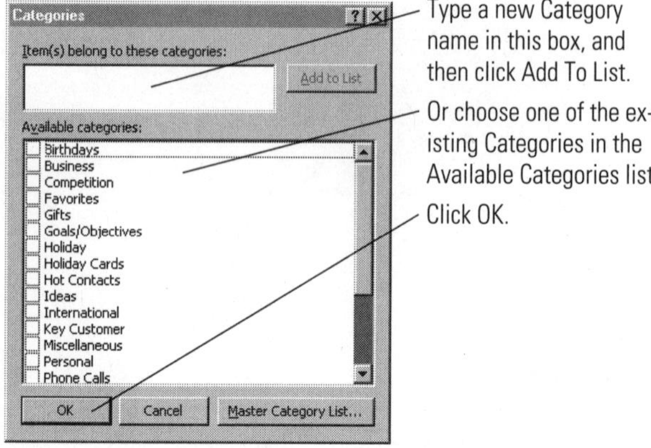

You can use the same procedure to assign tasks, contacts, appointments, and any other Outlook items to categories.

Using Categories to group tasks into projects

Outlook doesn't automatically group tasks into projects the way Schedule+ does, but that needn't stop you from using Outlook for basic project management. Just create a new category for each new project you start. For example, create a category called "Renovating the Bathroom." Thereafter, every time you add a new task associated with your bathroom renovation project, assign it to the new category. Then group tasks by category to collect all project tasks under the same heading.

Cc ❖ Copy

Character Formatting You can format characters in messages. Probably the easiest way to do it is by using the Formatting toolbar along the top of the Message form. The figure that follows points out where the Formatting toolbar is. I respectfully suggest that you experiment with these tools the next time you write a message.

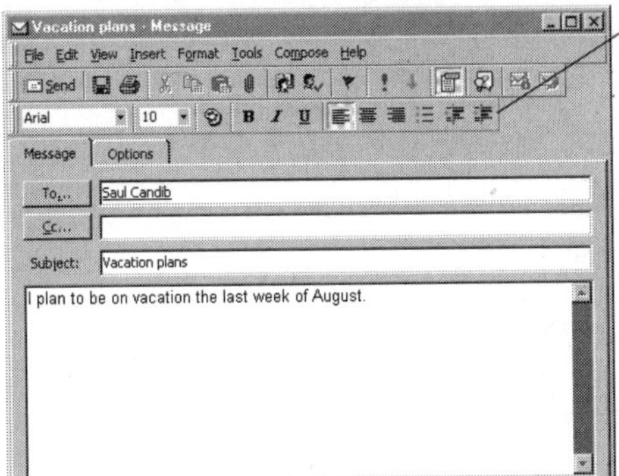

This is the Formatting toolbar.

Confused about which toolbar button is which?

When you move the mouse pointer over a toolbar button, Outlook displays a small pop-up box with the tool's name. If you forget which tool is which, you can use these pop-up boxes, called ToolTips, to jog your memory. Note, too, that whenever a menu command can be accessed by a toolbar button, that button's icon is displayed next to the command on the menu.

Alignment

Check Names You can verify that you've typed the names of message **recipients** correctly. To do this, choose Check Names from the Tools menu. (It appears on the Tools menu when the **Message form** is displayed.)

You don't have to type someone's entire name when you address an e-mail message, however—only enough of the name for Outlook to identify the recipient. When Saul sends a message addressed to "Steve" on our little **network,** for example, it gets to me even though the **Global Address List** shows my name as "Steve Nelson." And I can send a message back to "Saul" even though the Global Address List shows his name as "Saul Candib." When you click Check Names, Outlook replaces the partial name you entered with the full user name—provided it can match the partial name to a name on the Global Address List. On our network, for example, Outlook replaces "Steve" with "Steve Nelson." And it replaces "Saul" with "Saul Candib."

Spelling Checker

Client Local area networks (LANs) consist of two parts: clients and **servers.** If you're using Outlook as part of a LAN, the client part of the system (Outlook) runs on your computer; the server part (Microsoft Exchange Server), not surprisingly, runs on the server. The client part can function happily in either Windows 95 or Windows NT. We use Windows 95 for the **network** clients in our office, so all of the figures in this book look "Windows-95-ish." Your windows and dialog boxes might look different from ours if you use NT.

Outlook Client

Columns If you look closely at the right side of the Outlook window, you'll notice that it provides several pieces of information about the items listed, depending upon the particular **Outlook Folder** that's open. If the **Inbox** list is displayed, for example, icons identify messages that the **sender** flagged as important or that include an **attachment.** And the **information viewer** also identifies who sent the message and what its **subject** is.

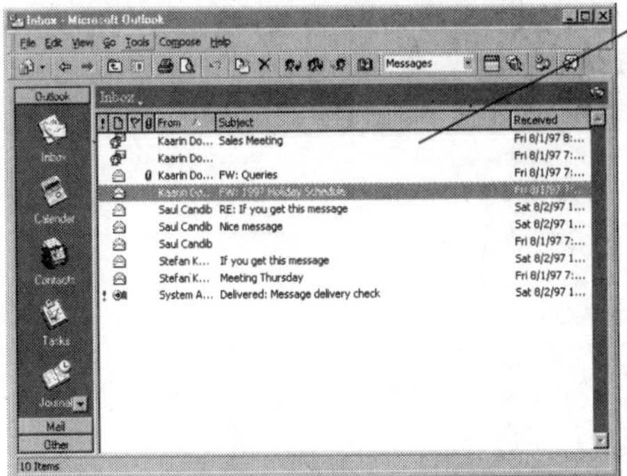

The Inbox information viewer provides several columns of information about messages.

You can decide for yourself which information the Inbox displays in its information viewer. To do so, choose Show Fields from the View menu and then use the boxes and buttons in the Show Fields dialog box to add and remove message information. To add message information to the information viewer, click an entry in the Available Fields box; then click Add. To remove message information, click an entry in the Show These Fields In This Order box; then click Remove.

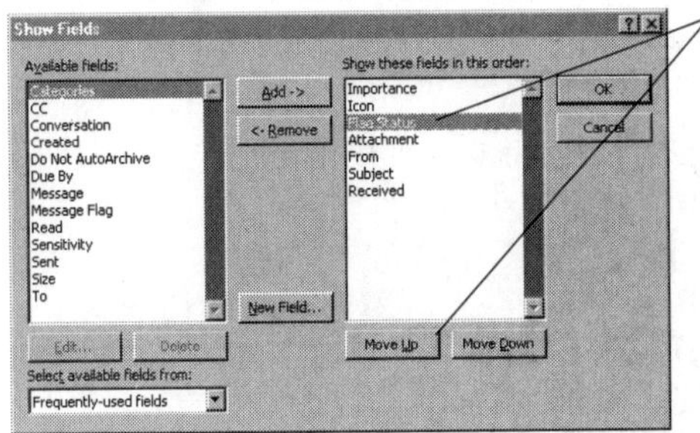

To change the position of a column, click it and then click the Move Up or Move Down button.

continues

Columns *(continued)*

The available fields in the Show Fields dialog box differ from one Outlook Folder to another. In the **Calendar,** for example, available fields include Location, Duration, and Recurrence Pattern. And in the Contact list, they include Job Title, Company, and Business Phone. You can customize the available fields using the list in the Select Available Fields From box.

Changing Column Formatting

You can format the columns that appear in a given view. To do so, choose Format Columns from the View menu.

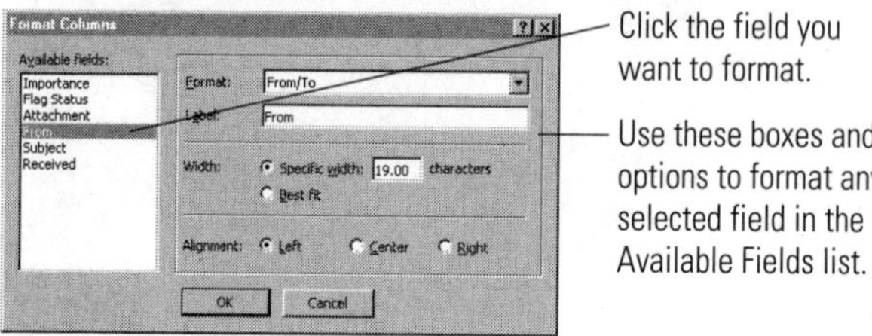

Click the field you want to format.

Use these boxes and options to format any selected field in the Available Fields list.

Fields

Contact List **Contacts**

Contacts

Contacts provides all you need in an electronic phone and address book, tracking nearly every conceivable kind of information about your friends and associates.

You enter contact information in the New Contact **form.** If your contacts are from large companies (or if they're just especially hip individuals), you can even include their **Web page** address and access it by clicking a toolbar button.

Like the other **Outlook Folders,** Contacts can be viewed in several different ways. Address Cards is a particularly cool **view**—it's like an electronic Rolodex file with a built-in index.

Adding a Contact to the Contact List

To add a new contact to the Contact list, choose New from the File menu and then choose Contact. Outlook displays the Untitled—Contact form.

Use these buttons and boxes to enter information about the contact's name, mailing address, job, and phone numbers.

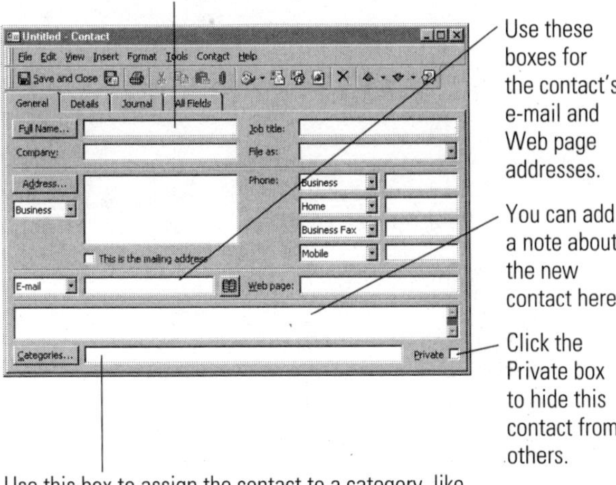

Use these boxes for the contact's e-mail and Web page addresses.

You can add a note about the new contact here.

Click the Private box to hide this contact from others.

Use this box to assign the contact to a category, like personal or business.

Changing the View of the Contact List

To change the view of the Contact list, first display the Contact list by clicking the Contacts icon in the Outlook Bar. Point to Current View on the View menu, and then choose a view from the list.

Use the Show Fields command on the View menu to reorder the fields in a view and to add new fields to a view. Use the Format View command to change the fonts and layout of a particular view. Use the Define Views command to add an entirely new view of your own design to the View list.

Looking Up a Contact in Address Cards View

Looking up a contact in Address Cards View is just like using a rotary file. You just spin the file, electronically, of course, until you find the card you want. First click Address Cards on the View Selector drop-down list.

continues

Contacts *(continued)*

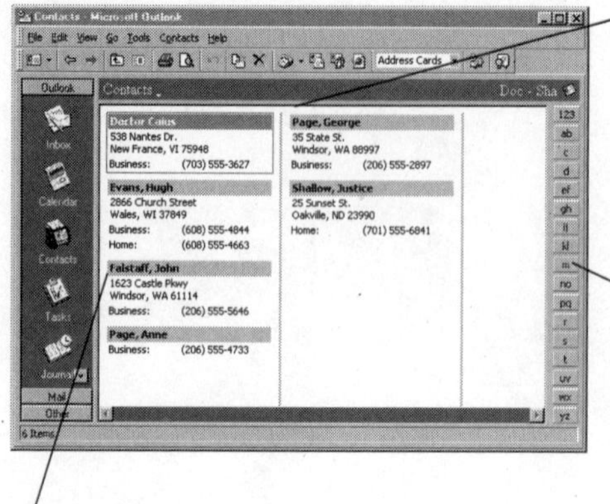

Address Cards view displays contacts as a list of Rolodex-like cards.

Click the index letter corresponding to the name of the contact you want to look up.

Double-click the name of the contact to display the Contact form.

Adding a Contact to Your E-Mail Address Book

You can tell Outlook to list contacts with e-mail or fax addresses in your **Address Book.** You'll then be able to send e-mail and faxes to those contacts merely by clicking the To button in the **Message form** and choosing the contact's name from the list in the Select Names dialog box.

First, however, you've got a little homework to do—you need to add the Outlook Address Book to your mail profile. Follow these steps:

1. Choose Services from the Tools menu.
2. In the Services dialog box, click Add.
3. Choose Outlook Address Book from the Available Information Services list in the Add Service To Profile dialog box.
4. Click OK twice.
5. Choose Exit And Log Off from the File menu.
6. The next time you log on to Outlook, you'll be able to use contact addresses.

Connecting with a contact quickly

Click the AutoDialer toolbar button to have your computer call the contact selected in your list. Click the New Message To Contact toolbar button to open a new Message form addressed to the selected contact. Click the New Meeting With Contact toolbar button to schedule an appointment with the selected contact. Click the Explore Web Page toolbar button to display the selected contact's World Wide Web home page.

AutoDial; Journal; Message

Conversation Thread A conversation thread is a **message** and all its **replies.** For example, if I send you an e-mail message that asks about a round of golf next Friday and you e-mail me a message saying that Friday doesn't work but Saturday sounds mighty fine, our two messages constitute a conversation thread.

Sometimes it's helpful to view the messages in a **folder** by conversation thread, so Outlook supplies a command called Group By that lets you do that. To use this view, simply choose Group By from the View menu and Outlook displays the Group By dialog box.

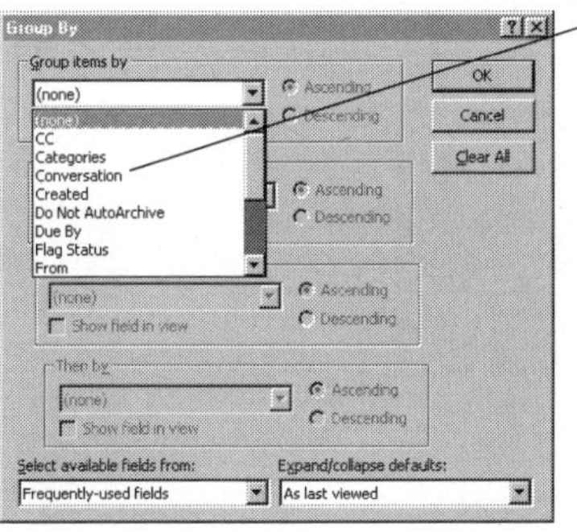

Choose Conversation from the list in the Group Items By drop-down list box.

Views

Copy You can send someone a copy of a **message** that you're sending to someone else. All you need to do is enter the person's **e-mail name** in the Cc box. Or if you don't know the person's e-mail name, click the Cc button. When Outlook displays the Select Names dialog box (which shows the contents of the **Address Book**), use it to identify the person to whom you want to send the copy.

Blind Carbon Copy

Custom Form Outlook allows you to create custom forms for collecting information from lots of different places. **Forms** sound funny at first, but they are actually very useful. You (or somebody else in your **organization**) might create an expense report form so that employees can describe and submit payment requests for reimbursable expenses. Or you might create a project status form so that the people working on a project can either report on or see how the project is progressing. You might even create a form that lets you share other, more entertaining information.

Date Navigator The Date Navigator is the small monthly calendar that appears in the upper right corner of the **Calendar** folder. You use the Date Navigator to pick the date or dates whose schedules are displayed in the Calendar.

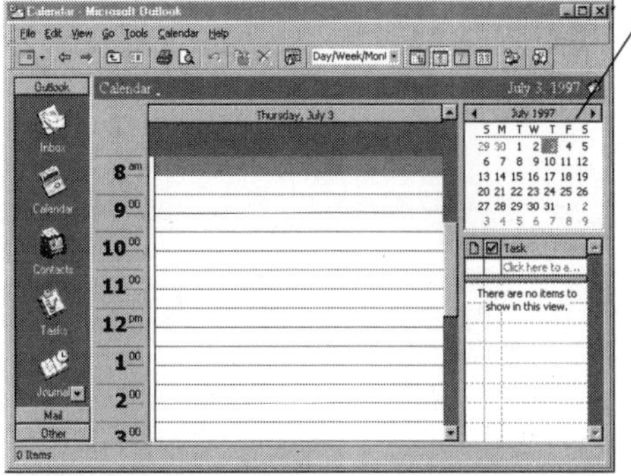

This is the Date Navigator.

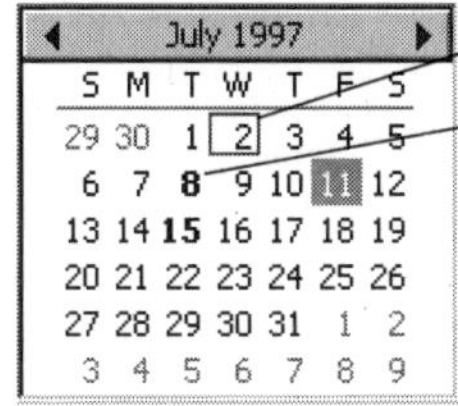

Today's date appears in a red square.

Days with scheduled activities appear in bold.

Schedules of selected dates are displayed in the Calendar.

Using the Date Navigator to Display Different Days' Schedules on the Calendar

Click a date to display that day's schedule in the Calendar. Drag the pointer over a series of dates to select them all, or select nonadjacent dates by holding down the CTRL key and clicking each date.

Moving From One Month to Another in Date Navigator

Click the left arrow to display the previous month; click the right arrow to display the next month. Click the month name in the Date Navigator's title bar, and a list of month names appears. Move the pointer over one of the month names and release the mouse button to display that month in the Date Navigator.

continues

Date Navigator *(continued)*

Rescheduling an Appointment Using the Date Navigator

Simply drag a scheduled appointment from the Calendar to a date in the Date Navigator to reschedule the appointment for a different day.

Appointment

Defining Views Views

Delegate Access Permissions

When you're using Outlook as an Exchange client, delegate access permissions specify who can do what with the appointment **Calendar**. The default delegate access permission setting is for other people to be able to view your **Meeting Planner**. When others can view your Meeting Planner, they can see when you are busy and when you are free (and they can suggest meeting times). You can, however, give other users much greater control over your schedule—even to the point of scheduling meetings for you, reviewing private **appointments** and **tasks**, and sending and receiving **e-mail** on your behalf.

To make changes like these to Outlook delegate access permissions, choose Options from the Tools menu and click the Delegates tab. Before you start fooling around with these settings, however, you might just want to check with your network **administrator** to see whether your company has policies regarding delegate access permissions. It probably does.

Delivery Receipt The United States Postal Service, as you might know, offers a special service called "registered mail." With registered mail, you get a delivery receipt, signed by the recipient, to prove that your letter or package truly reached its destination. Microsoft Exchange Server provides a similar service with its delivery receipts. You can ask Exchange Server to confirm that a **message** was delivered. To do this, choose Properties from the File menu in the Message form before you send the message and then click the General tab.

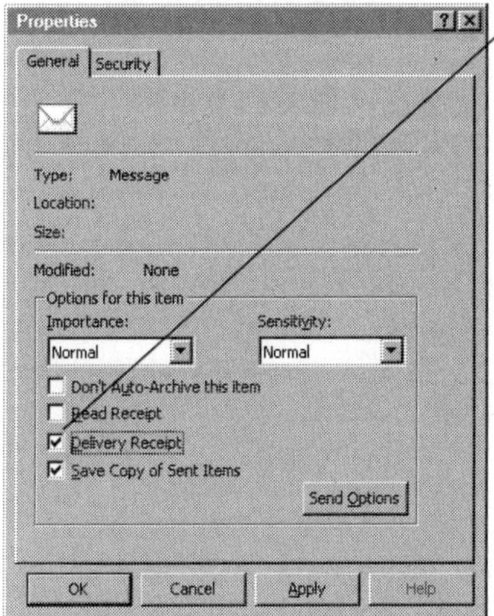

Click the Delivery Receipt check box to ask Exchange Server to tell you when it finishes delivering a message.

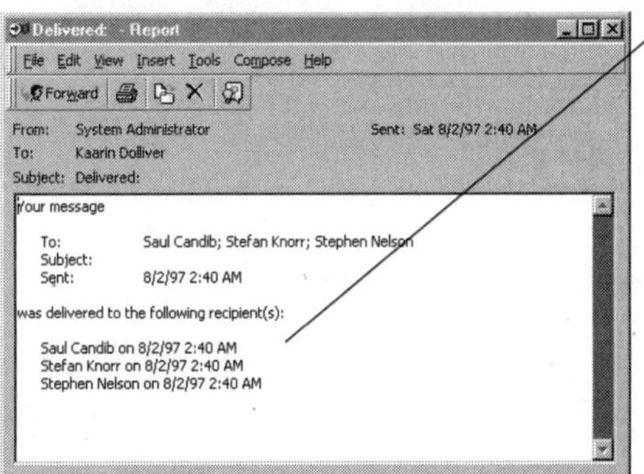

This is the message you'll receive that confirms the delivery of your message.

Read Receipt

Digital Signature Have you ever seen one of those sealing wax kits? Mostly, I think, kids use them now. But a long time ago, the kings and queens of Europe used them to seal their messages. They dripped hot wax over the envelope flap and then made an impression on the soft wax with their signet rings. When recipients received the letters, they could tell right away that they came from, for example, the Holy Roman Emperor. All they had to do was look at the impression made by the ring. What's more, they could tell whether the letter had been tampered with by seeing if the wax was still in place.

Digital signatures work in a similar manner. They seal and sign a **message** so that its **recipient** can tell who the message really came from and be certain that no one tampered with the message en route.

Signing a Message with a Digital Signature

To add a digital signature to a message, click the Digitally Sign Message button on the Message toolbar and click Send after you've finished composing your message. To use digital signatures, both the sender and recipient must have Advanced Security turned on. Type your security password in the Password box.

Verifying a Digital Signature

To verify that a message with a digital signature is real and that it hasn't been tampered with, choose Properties from the File menu when the message shows. Then click the Security tab, and click the Verify Digital Signature To Message button.

Security

Discussions **Post Message**

Distribution List A distribution list is just a group of people to whom you want to send a **message.** That sounds like no big deal, but distribution lists are actually pretty neat because they make it easy to send a message to a bunch of people. Rather than separately listing the name of each **recipient** to whom you want to send a message, you just specify the distribution list.

Creating a Distribution List

As long as you've already added the recipients to your **Personal Address Book** or you can find the recipients in the **Global Address List,** it's easy to create a long distribution list. To create the list, follow these steps:

1 Display the Address Book by clicking the Address Book button. Outlook displays the Address Book dialog box.

2 Click the New Entry button. Outlook displays the New Entry dialog box.

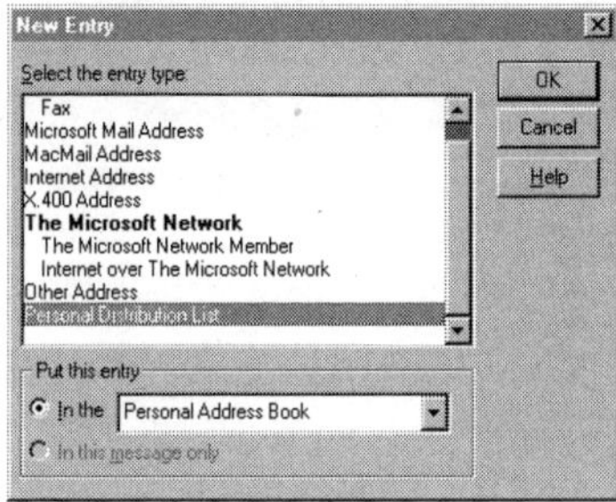

3 Double-click the Personal Distribution List entry. Outlook displays the New Personal Distribution List Properties dialog box.

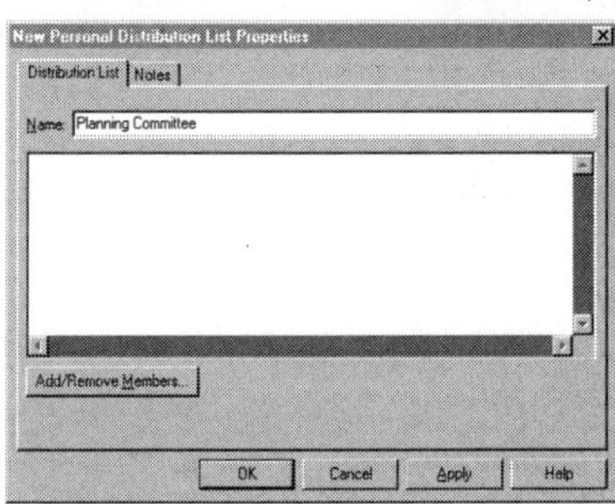

4 Name the personal distribution list by entering a brief description in the Name box.

5 Click the Add/Remove Members button. Outlook displays the Edit New Personal Distribution List Members dialog box.

6 Double-click the **e-mail names** of the people you want to add to the personal distribution list.

Using a Distribution List

To send the same e-mail message to everyone named on a distribution list, just enter the distribution list name in the To box of the **Message form**.

Domain Domain is really a Windows NT term, but it isn't hard to understand. A domain is a collection of **servers** and **clients** that get administered together. A Windows NT **network** can have a single domain (usually the case with small networks). Or it can have a bunch of different domains (usually the case with big or geographically dispersed networks).

In case you are an **Internet** user, I should probably tell you one other thing: Windows NT domains aren't the same as Internet domains. And this is confusing, because if you add an Internet mail address to your **Address Book**, Outlook asks for the Internet domain name.

Organization; Site

Electronic Mail **E-Mail**

E-Mail E-mail is an abbreviation that stands for electronic mail. The term describes the **messages** that people send from one computer to another. In most cases, e-mail is transmitted instantaneously—or almost instantaneously. You send a message, and, a few seconds or minutes later, someone receives it.

E-Mail Alias An e-mail alias is usually the same thing as an **e-mail name.** It's the name you use to send someone an e-mail message.

E-Mail Etiquette Good manners are never complicated, so you won't be surprised to learn that there's nothing particularly tricky about the etiquette of e-mail. Be courteous. Never say something you don't want repeated (or forwarded). Don't waste your recipient's time by sending useless messages or replies. In short, treat people as you yourself want to be treated, and respect their time.

E-Mail Filters ⁘ **Inbox Filters**

E-Mail Name If you want to send me an e-mail **message,** you can't just type "Stephen L. Nelson" in the To box. My name might mean a lot to me, but to Outlook and the Internet, my name means hardly anything. What Outlook and the Internet use to uniquely identify me is my e-mail name. StphnLNlson, my e-mail name on The Microsoft Network, does mean something. And if you sent an e-mail message to the Internet address StphnLNlsn@msn.com, it would actually get to me. I might even read it. (I'm joking. Of course I'd read it.)

Embedding and Linking Existing Objects To create an **OLE** object from an existing **file,** display the **Message form,** position the insertion point where you want to insert the new object, and follow these steps:

1 From the Insert menu, choose Object.

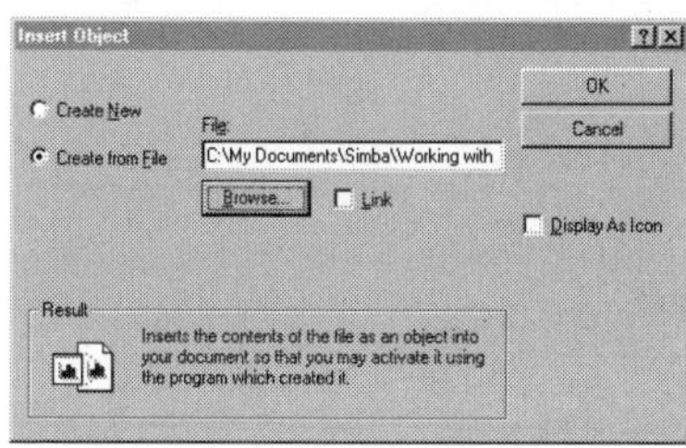

2 Click Create From File.

3 If you know the filename and path of the object, type it in the File box and go straight to step 8. Otherwise, go to step 4.

continues

Embedding and Linking Existing Objects *(continued)*

4 Click the Browse button.

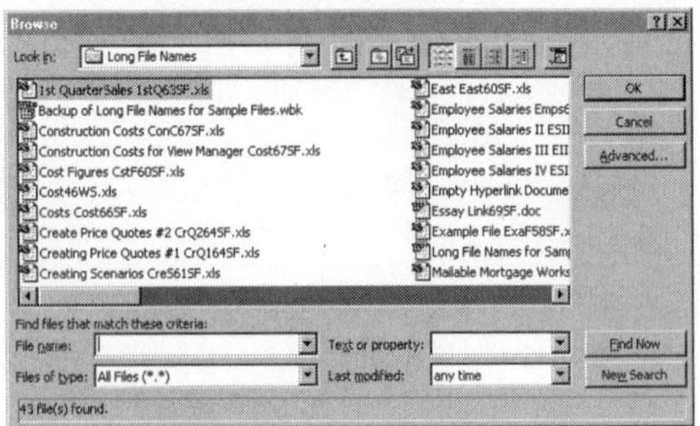

5 Use the Files Of Type box to specify the type of file you're looking for.

6 Use the Up One Level toolbar button, the Look In box, and the list of **folders** beneath it to identify the folder where the file is located.

7 Click the file, and then click OK.

8 Back in the Insert Object dialog box, check the Link box if you want Windows 95 to automatically update the object whenever changes are made to the original file.

9 Check the Display As Icon box if you want Outlook to display the object as an icon rather than displaying the contents of the file.

10 Click OK.

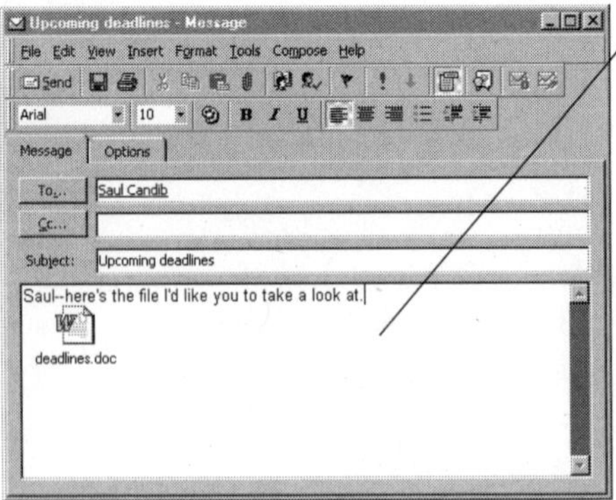

Here's a message form with an object I inserted.

Embedding New Objects To create a new **OLE** object from scratch, follow these steps:

1 From the Insert menu, choose Object.

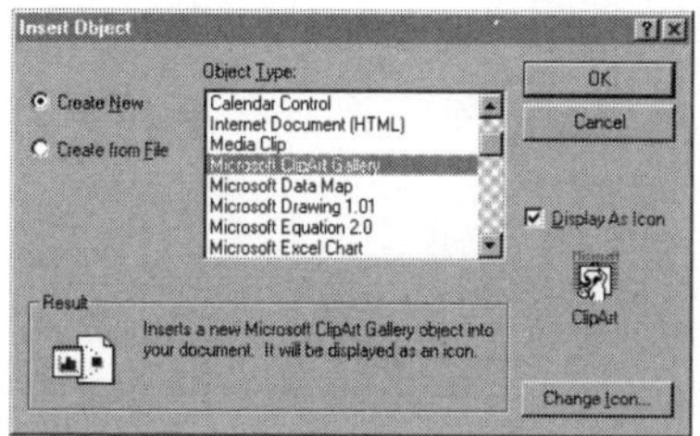

2 Select the Windows program in which you will create the object.

3 Check the Display As Icon box to see the object as an icon rather than as a picture.

4 Click OK. Outlook starts the selected **program,** allowing you to create the object.

5 Click anywhere on the message form outside the object to embed the object.

Encryption When you encrypt something—like an e-mail **message**—you scramble the information so that it can't be read by anyone who doesn't know how to unscramble it. When the **recipient** gets your e-mail message, he or she decrypts, or unscrambles, it in order to read it.

Event In Outlook an event is a notation in the **Calendar** that doesn't occupy a time slot. This sounds funny, but take the example of a child's birthday. You might want to note this event on your calendar—so you remember to buy a gift, say—even though the event doesn't actually take time out of your work day. To put it another way, events are occasions that you want to remember but not necessarily schedule time for.

continues

Event *(continued)*

Creating an Event

To add an event to your Calendar, click the Calendar icon in the Outlook Bar. From the Calendar menu, choose New Event. Then use the Event dialog box to describe the event and its timing.

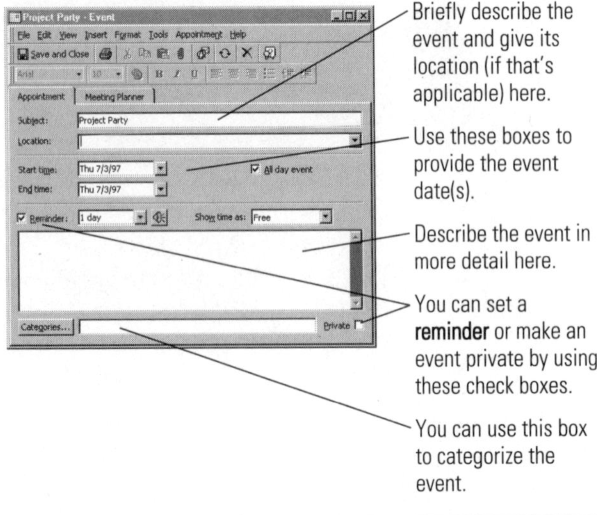

Viewing Event Information

You can view event information in several ways. Outlook doesn't block out time on your Calendar for events. Events appear on the Calendar as notices above the day or days they are scheduled. You can also click Events in the Current View box to see a list of all the scheduled events.

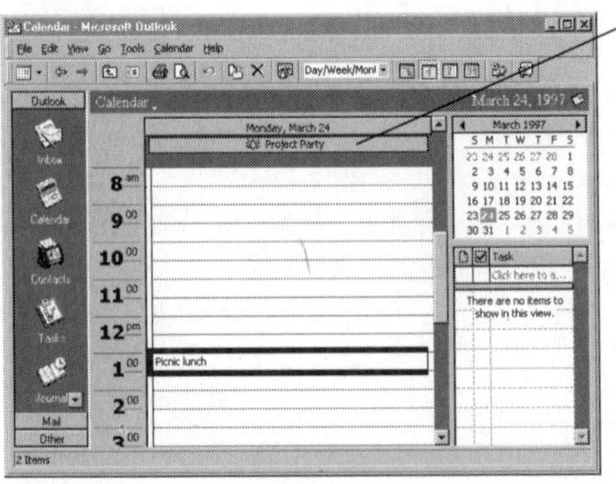

On the daily Calendar, all day events show up here.

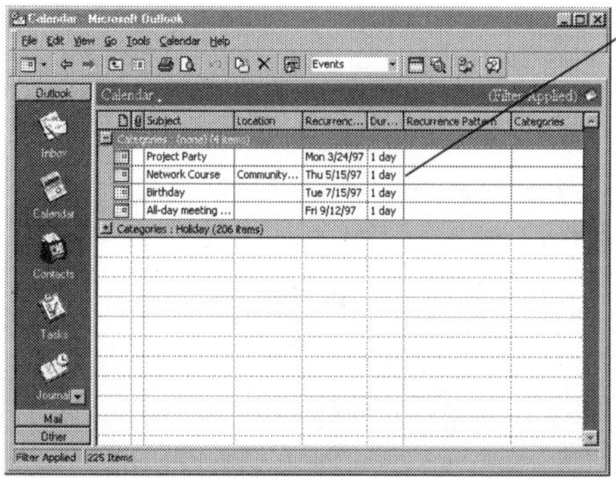

When you choose Events View, all of your scheduled events show up in a list.

Favorites Folder The Favorites folder, a subfolder in the Windows folder, is a place where you can store files, shortcuts, or even other folders that you use frequently, so you know where to find them. In addition, your Internet browser stores your favorite **URLs** in the Favorites folder. Outlook provides a quick way to get to your Favorites folder. Just click the built-in Favorites icon on the Outlook Bar.

Other Folders

Field Chooser **Fields**

Fields Outlook provides a variety of fields to describe details of particular **items.** You can add and remove fields from **views** of Outlook items. You can also create entirely new fields of your own.

In views that list items in a table format, such as the Messages view of the **Inbox,** fields are the **columns** of the table. In other types of views (such as the Address Cards view of the **Contact list**), fields can appear as rows.

continues

Fields *(continued)*

Changing the Fields in a View

To change the fields displayed in a view, choose Show Fields from the View menu. Outlook displays the Show Fields dialog box.

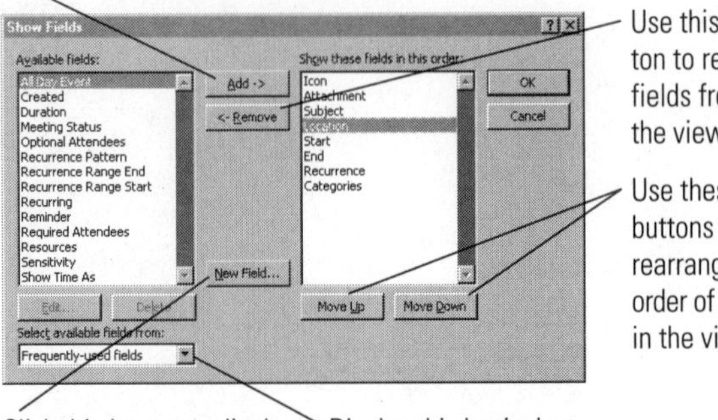

Using the Field Chooser

The Field Chooser lets you add and remove fields just like the Show Fields command, but in a more visual fashion—by simply dragging and dropping fields to and from the column headings area of the view. It's pretty neat. Try it!

To display the Field Chooser, choose Field Chooser from the View menu.

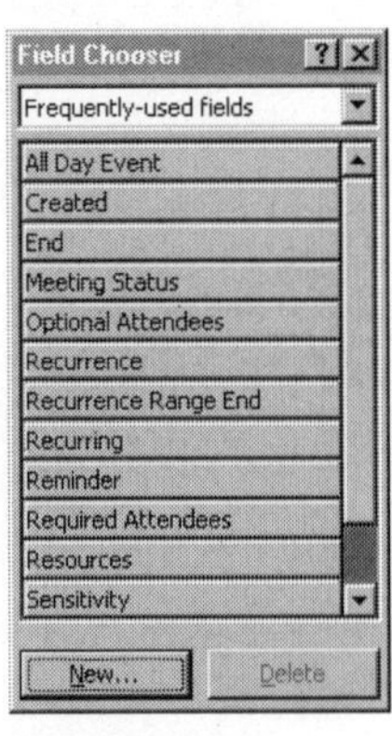

To add a field to the current view, drag a field from the Field Chooser to the place you want it to appear in the column headings of the view.

Group By Box; Views

File

A file is what you (and the computer **programs** you use) store on your computer's hard disk. As important as your departmental budget may be to you, to your computer it's just another file—the same as any other. That novel you've been slaving away on for the last 11 years? Another file. You get the picture.

As far as Outlook goes, you need to know two things about files: you can attach files to the **messages** you send, and you can make it easier to share files that a whole bunch of people need to work with by plopping them into **public folders.**

Post Messages

File Extensions

In MS-DOS and the earlier versions of Windows, you stuck a three-letter file extension at the end of file names. The file extension identified the file type. Because of this history, many of the **files** you see on a **network** use a file extension to identify the file type.

Name	Size
Adding a Header and Footer.pot	31KB
Adding and Deleting Slides.pot	102KB
Adjusting Heights and Widths..xlt	15KB
Building a Table.doc	13KB
Business Contacts.mdb	176KB
Changing Color Schemes.pot	85KB
Creating a Database File.doc	13KB

The three-letter string following the period is the file extension.

Filters

Filters allow you to choose the items you want to display in the **information viewer.** Filters narrow down the list of items in a folder to just the ones that meet criteria you set. To filter items, you use the Filter command on the View menu.

When you choose Filter from the View menu in the **Calendar** folder, for example, Outlook displays the Filter dialog box.

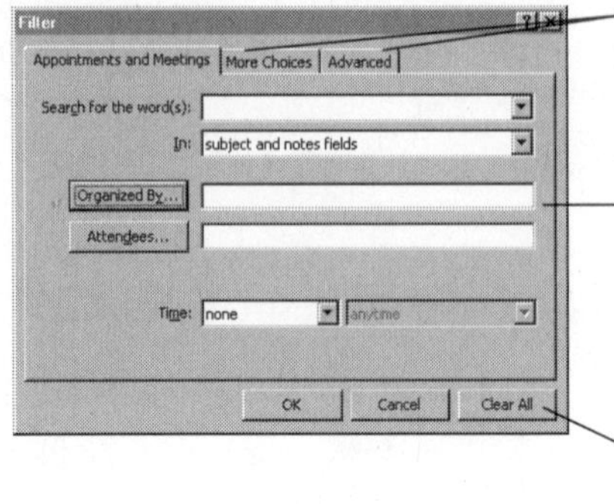

Use the More Choices and Advanced tabs to establish additional search criteria.

Use these buttons and boxes to find the appointments and meetings that meet your criteria.

Click this button to remove all filters and display the entire contents of the selected folder.

Outlook reminds you that you've filtered the information viewer by adding the words "Filter Applied" to the folder title bar.

 **Inbox Filters; Task Filters; Views**

Find

I don't get many **e-mail messages** in a day. Maybe one or two at the most. And my **contacts** list is rather short. Furthermore, I try to keep my **tasks** list under control. So I usually don't have too much trouble locating **items.**

But if you work in a large **organization** where everybody has e-mail, or if you maintain a long contacts list, or if you're a manager who's constantly assigning tasks and attending meetings, the volume of items you need to track can be staggering. In such an environment, it's easy to lose or misplace items of importance.

Fortunately, Outlook provides a powerful Find tool you can use to locate lost messages, tasks, contacts, and other items. To use this tool, choose Find Items from the Tools menu. You use its buttons and boxes to describe the item or items you are looking for. After you provide a description, you click the Find Now button. Outlook lists any items that match your description in a list at the bottom of the window.

Specify the type of item you are looking for.

Click Browse to tell Outlook exactly where to look for it.

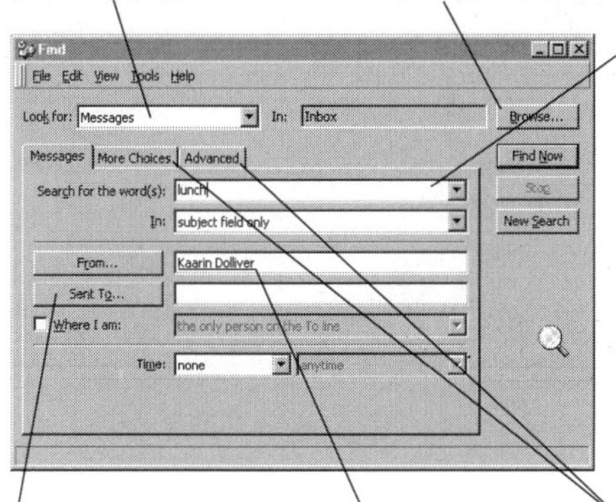

Enter any specific words or phrases that you think will help in the search, using semicolons to separate multiple entries.

Use the Sent To box, the Where I Am check box, and the text box next to it to search for messages sent directly to you or only **copied** to you.

Enter the **sender** name or recipient name, using semicolons to separate multiple **e-mail names**.

Use the More Choices and Advanced tabs to make the search more specific.

About the More Choices and Advanced tabs

You can specify additional search criteria by clicking the Advanced button and using the Advanced tab options. These options, for example, let you tell Outlook to look for messages with **attachments,** messages of a certain size, and messages that fit in one of the **categories** you have assigned.

continues

Find *(continued)*

Finding Outlook Items Using the Start Menu

When you installed Outlook, Windows added a new command to the Find submenu on your Start menu: Using Microsoft Outlook. When you choose this command, Windows displays the Find dialog box so you can search for Outlook items from anywhere in your computer without having to launch Outlook.

Finding Message Text

When you're writing or reading a message, you can use the Find command on the Edit menu to locate words, phrases, or other fragments of text in the message. To find text in a message, select the part of the message you want to search. If you want to search the entire message, don't select anything. Then click Find on the Edit menu.

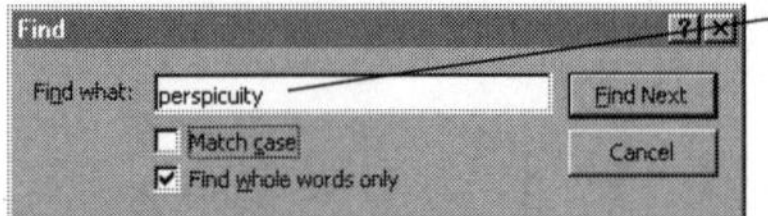

Specify what it is you're looking for.

Use the Match Case and Find Whole Words Only check boxes to tell Outlook to consider case (lowercase vs. uppercase) in its search and look only for whole words rather than parts of words.

Flame

A flame is an **e-mail message** that's mean and nasty. If you e-mail a message to me that says I'm a complete moron who is utterly incapable of constructing a sentence, for example, that's a flame. By the way, if I e-mail you back a message that says your mother wears army boots and your sister is ugly, we have what is known as a "flame war."

Flames, as you might guess, violate all the rules of e-mail good manners and etiquette. But because some people have the maturity of grade-schoolers, you see quite a few flames—particularly on the **Internet**. On a philosophical note, I suspect that the anonymity of e-mail and the Internet has something to do with this meanness. People are more apt to say mean and threatening things when they don't have to see the other person's face or worry about running into the other person at the grocery store or a staff meeting.

Folder

In Windows, your disks and the **files** they store are organized into folders. (Folders, by the way, replace MS-DOS's directories.) What's more, folders can be stored within other folders. And now I want to share my only published poem with you:

Monkey see, monkey do.

Windows uses folders,

So Outlook does too.

By the way, it's easy to create new folders. Select the folder or mailbox into which you want to place a new folder. Then choose New from the File menu and Folder from the submenu. Or choose Folder from the File menu and then Create Subfolder from the submenu. When Outlook displays the Create New Folder dialog box, name the new folder, and click OK.

Folder List; Outlook Folders; Subfolder

Folder Banner The Folder Banner is the bar below the toolbars in the Outlook window. On the left side of the Folder Banner, Outlook displays the name of the selected folder. You can click the folder name to display a list of all **Outlook folders.** The Folder Banner also displays the selected folder's icon and additional information such as today's date in **Calendar** or the alphabetical range of contacts displayed in **Contacts.**

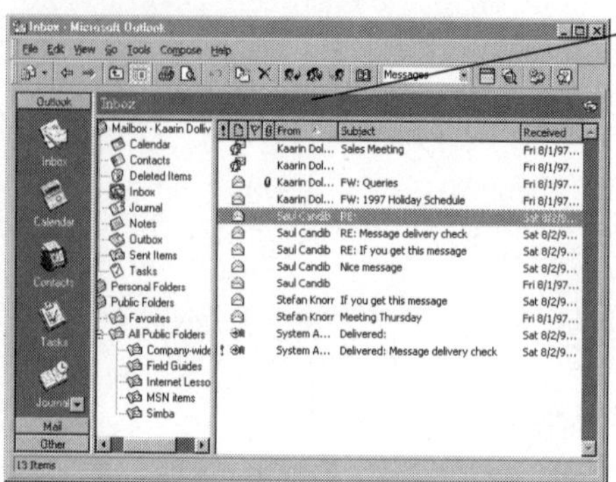

This is the Folder Banner.

Folder List The term *folder list* refers to the left half of the Outlook window where Outlook displays the folder tree, or hierarchy. If you've worked with Outlook for more than a day or two, you already know that Outlook uses these **folders** to organize various **items.** Among the folders in the Folder List are the **Inbox, Calendar, Contacts,** and **Journal.** In addition, you can use Outlook just like you'd use Windows Explorer or My Computer—to display the folder hierarchy of your entire computer and network.

If the Folder List doesn't appear in the Outlook program window and you want to see it, choose Folder List from the View menu, or click the Folder List toolbar button.

Outlook Folders

Folder View A folder view is a certain way to look at the information in a specific **folder**. For example, you can organize the **messages** in the **Inbox** folder by specifying which **columns** (or **fields**) appear, how messages are grouped or sorted, and whether any **e-mail filters** are used. Outlook doesn't offer predefined folder **views,** but you can create your own customized views by choosing Define Views from the View menu.

Creating a Folder View

To create a folder view, choose Define Views from the View menu. When Outlook displays the Define Views dialog box, click the New button. Outlook displays the Create A New View dialog box.

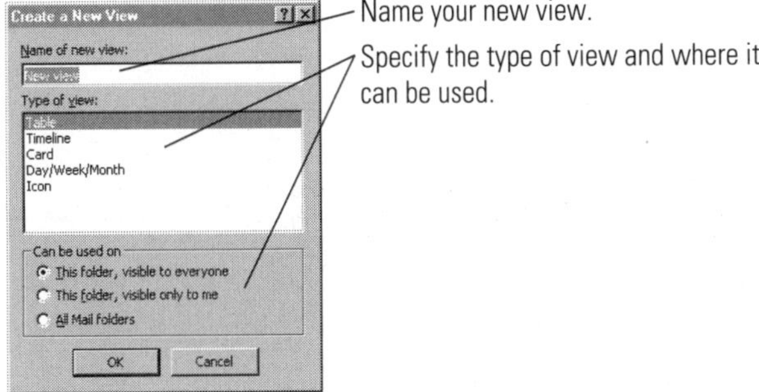

When you click OK, Outlook displays the View Summary dialog box.

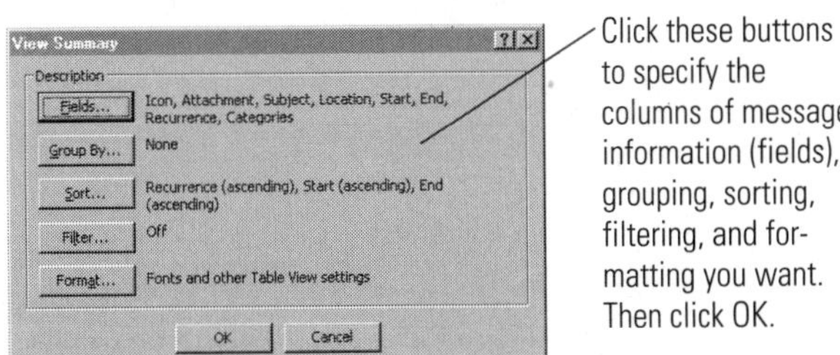

Using a Folder View

To use a folder view after you create it, choose Current Views from the View menu and then choose a view from the submenu.

Fields; Grouping Messages; Sorting

Font

If you've worked with a word processor—say, **Microsoft Word**—you probably know that a font is simply a typeface that looks a certain way. What you may not know is that because Outlook happily passes back and forth what are called Rich Text Format (RTF) files, it lets you include all sorts of fonts in messages.

Be careful about mixing and matching too many fonts, unless you want to get the infamous "ransom note" look.

It's easy to format a **message.** With the **Message form** displayed, select the text and then choose Font from the Format menu. When Outlook displays the Font dialog box, use it to make your formatting changes.

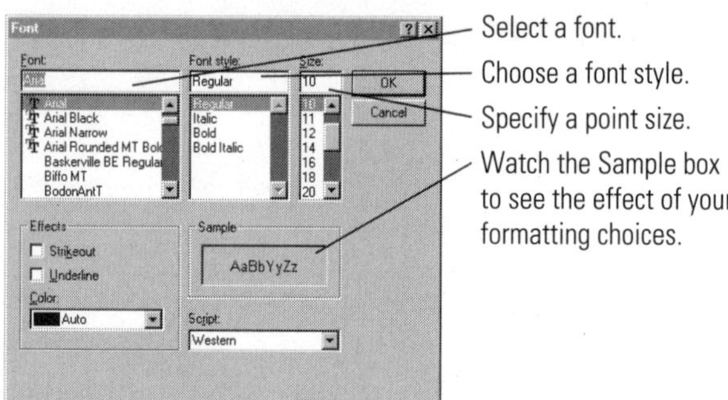

Form

In Outlook, you use forms to collect and view information. For example, when you create a **message,** you use a form called, cleverly enough, the **Message form.** In this form you name the **recipient,** the message **subject,** and type in the **message body**. Outlook comes with predefined forms for writing and reading **e-mail** messages, of course. But you can create specialized forms for collecting and viewing other types of information, too: employee expense reports, project schedule updates, and so on.

Custom Form

Form Design You can use Outlook's Design Outlook Forms command to create your own customized **forms.** This book doesn't cover form design in any detail because, alas, there isn't enough space. If you want more information about form design, however, consult *Microsoft Exchange in Business* (Microsoft Press, 1996). It describes how to create customized forms. You can order a copy by calling (800) MSPRESS. (International callers need to precede this telephone number with the appropriate international access and country codes.)

Custom Form

Forward You can send a copy of a **message** you receive to someone else. To do this, select or display the message and then click the Forward toolbar button. Outlook opens a **form** that you use to create your response.

Free Time **Busy Time**

Global Address List The Global Address List lists all the people in your **organization** to whom you can send mail. The GAL, as people who revel in political incorrectness call it, can be viewed by clicking the Address Book toolbar button and then clicking Global Address List in the Show Names From The list.

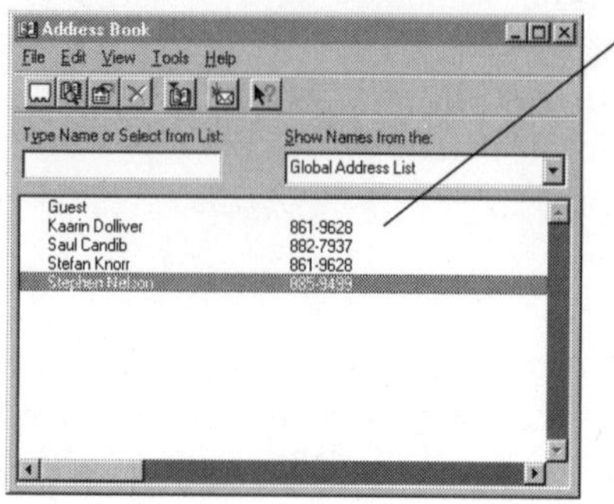

We're a small business with only a handful of regular employees, so our Global Address List shows only five names: Kaarin's, Saul's, Stefan's, mine, and one for a generic "Guest" user.

If your organization is huge, with hundreds or thousands of **users,** the Global Address List isn't a useful way to find the **e-mail names** of people you correspond with regularly. Instead, add your regular correspondents' e-mail names to your **Personal Address Book.**

Group By Box The easiest way to group and ungroup **messages** and **tasks** is to use the Group By box. When you choose Group By Box from the View menu or click Group By Box on the toolbar, Outlook opens a space between the **Folder Banner** and the column headings of the **information viewer.** You can drag column headings in and out of the Group By box to group items by those headings. Outlook groups items based on the order in which the headings appear in the box. If you don't like the order, simply rearrange the headings. And when you want to ungroup items, just drag the headings back into the column heading area.

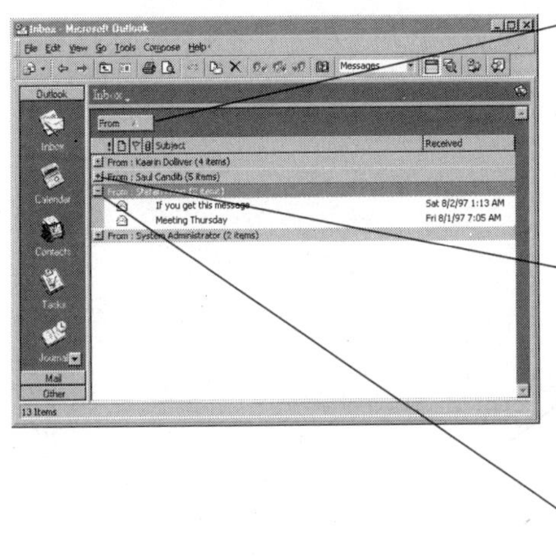

I dragged the From heading into the Group By box to group all messages by Sender.

Click a plus sign to expand a group and view the messages it contains.

Expanded groups are indicated by minus signs.

Grouping Messages; Views

Grouping Messages You can tell Outlook to group **messages** with similar characteristics—the same **sender,** the same **subject,** and so on. To do this, choose Group By from the View menu. When Outlook displays the Group By dialog box, use its boxes and buttons to specify how you want to group messages.

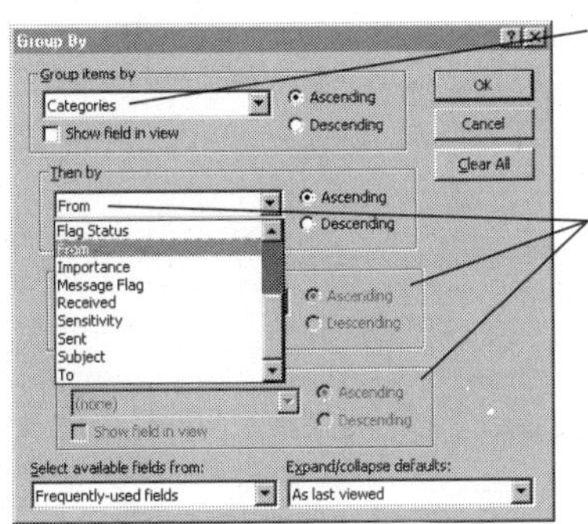

Specify how you want messages grouped by using the Group Items By drop-down list box.

You can group messages within a group by using the Then By list boxes.

continues

Grouping Messages *(continued)*

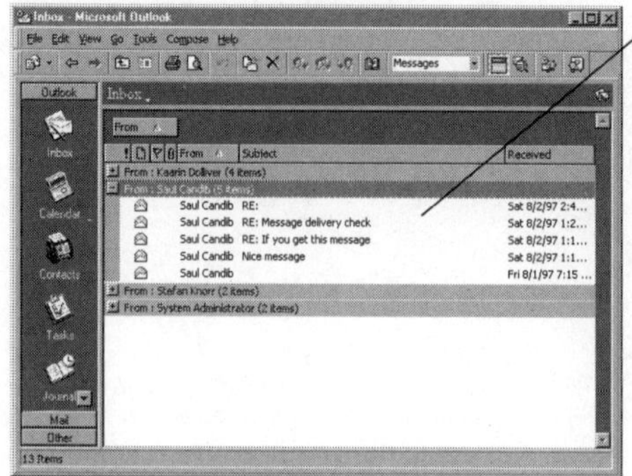

This **information viewer** groups messages by sender.

Working with groups

If you group your messages, you ought to know about the Expand/Collapse All command on the View menu. Collapse All shows your message groups but hides the individual messages in a group. Expand All, in effect, "uncollapses" a group.

Group By Box

Help

Outlook's online Help feature gives you information with just a click or keystroke. You can access the conventional Help system by choosing Contents and Index from the Help menu. But Outlook also uses Microsoft Office's new Help feature: clicking the Help toolbar button or choosing Microsoft Outlook Help from the Help menu displays the **Office Assistant,** an animated Help guru.

HTML The acronym HTML stands for hypertext markup language. HTML is what you use to create **World Wide Web** documents. In fact, for this reason the HTML acronym is often used as the last part of a World Wide Web document name—to identify what it is. (On PCs, World Wide Web documents use the file extension .htm for the same basic reason.) Do you need to know this? No, not really. The only time you'd ever even need to worry about or work with HTML is if you were creating your own World Wide Web documents.

Hyperlink You can put a link to a **World Wide Web** page or FTP site—a hyperlink—in your **messages**. You just need to know the **URL**, or hyperlink address, of the **Web page** or FTP site to which you want to link. To insert a hyperlink into a message, type the hyperlink address in the message area of the **Message form.**

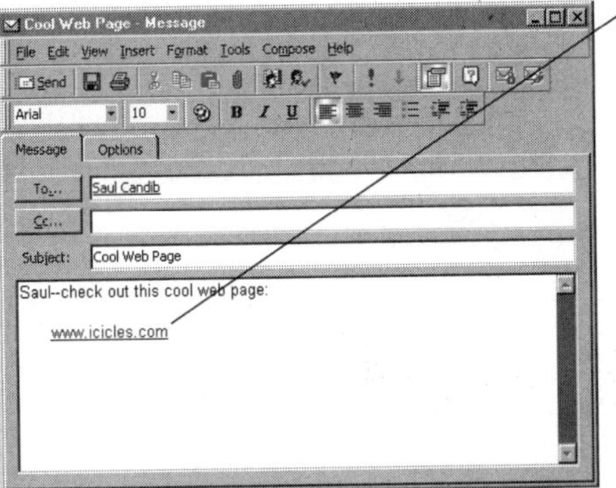

This is the hyperlink to a Web page.

If you have a **Web browser,** you can take advantage of the URL addresses stored in your **Favorites** folder to insert a shortcut to a Web page into your messages. Just click in the message area of the Message form. Then choose File from the Insert menu. In the Insert File dialog box, click the Look In Favorites toolbar button. Make sure that Attachment is selected under Insert As. Double-click the URL you want to insert into your message.

continues

Hyperlink *(continued)*

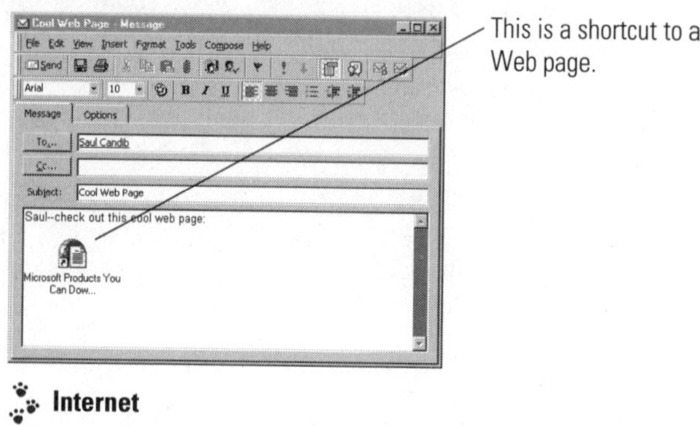

Internet

Importance Some of the **messages** you send are very important either to you or the **recipient**. And some of the messages aren't important at all. To deal with differences in urgency and importance, you can assign a priority, or level of importance, to the messages you write. Unless you tell it otherwise, Outlook assumes your message is of normal importance. To assign high importance to a message, click the Importance: High toolbar button. To assign low importance, click the (you guessed it) Importance: Low toolbar button.

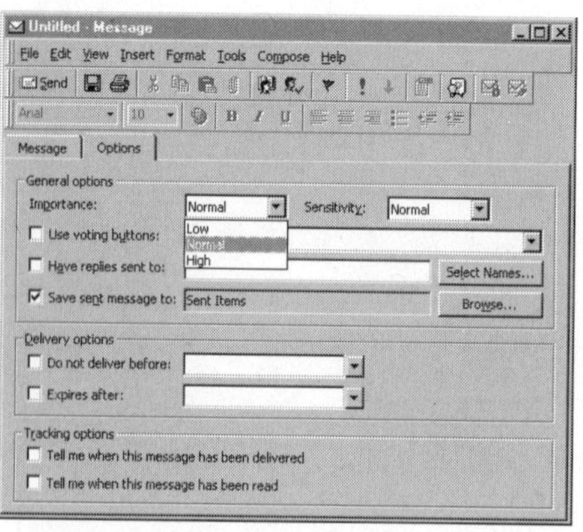

The importance level shows up in the recipient's **information viewer,** which theoretically helps the recipient identify urgent and important messages. By the way, Microsoft Exchange Server can be set up to deliver high-priority messages faster.

Import And Export Outlook provides the Import And Export Wizard to help you import items and files from other applications into Outlook and export items and files from Outlook to other applications. For example, if you have a file in another personal information manager that contains names and addresses of business contacts, you can use the Import And Export Wizard to move that information into Outlook. If you're moving to Outlook from Schedule+, you can import Schedule+ files into Outlook.

Importing Contacts from Schedule+

To import a contact file from Schedule+, follow these steps:

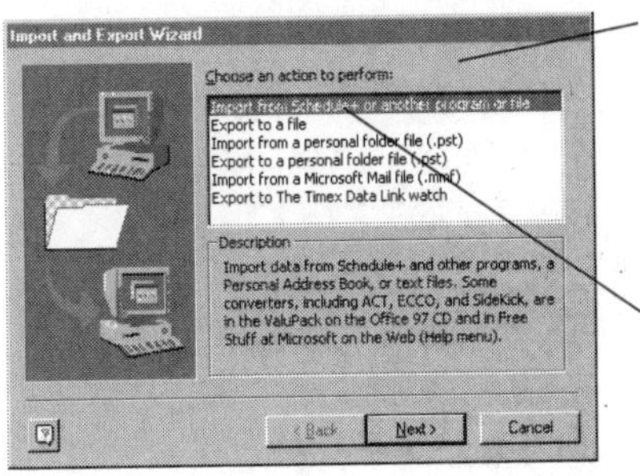

1 Choose Import And Export from the File menu. Outlook displays the Import And Export dialog box.

2 Select Import From Schedule+ Or Another Application Or File in the Choose An Action To Perform list box. Then click Next. Outlook displays the Import A File dialog box.

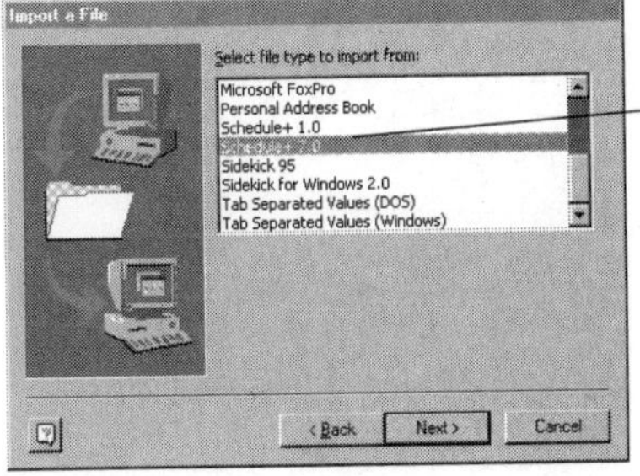

3 Select Schedule+ 7.0 in the Select File Type To Import From box. Click Next, and Outlook displays the next Import A File dialog box.

continues

Import And Export *(continued)*

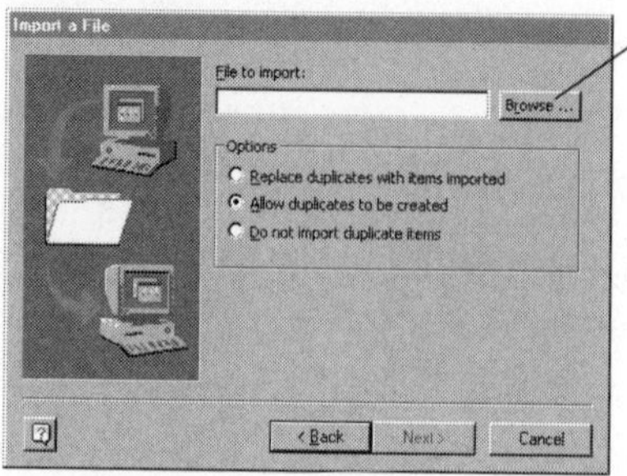

4 Click Browse to find the Schedule+ file on your hard disk. It will have the file extension .SCD.

5 In the final Import A File dialog box, check to make sure that Outlook will import the files you want. Click Finish.

Calendar; Contacts; Schedule+

Inbox

The Inbox is just the **Outlook Folder** that receives and holds incoming **messages.** To view your Inbox, click the Inbox folder icon in the **Folder List** or the Inbox icon in the **Outlook Bar.**

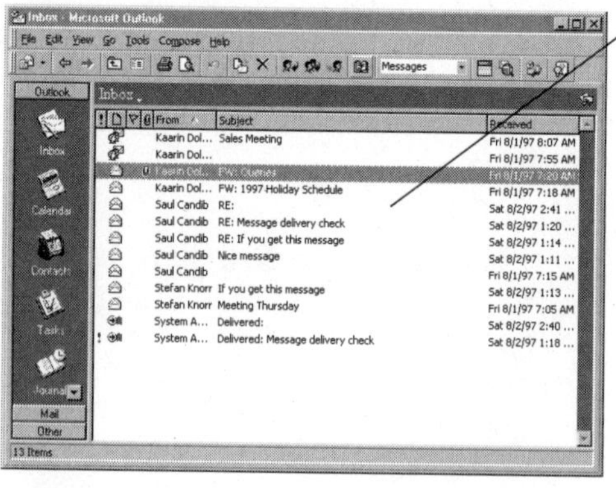

The Inbox folder lists all of the messages that other people have sent.

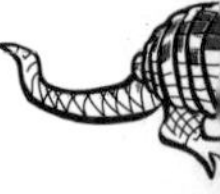

Inbox Assistant The Inbox Assistant from Microsoft Exchange is no longer with us. You can use the **Rules Wizard** to perform all the same functions that you once relied upon the Inbox Assistant to perform.

Out Of Office Assistant

Inbox Filters You can filter, or weed out, the **messages** that appear in the **information viewer** so that only messages with specific characteristics appear. For example, you can filter the information viewer so that only messages from particular (or even peculiar) **senders** get listed. Or you can filter messages so that only those marked as important or those with **attachments** get listed.

To filter messages, select the **folder** with the messages you want to filter. Then choose Filter from the View menu. Outlook displays the Filter dialog box, which you use to describe how you want to filter the messages.

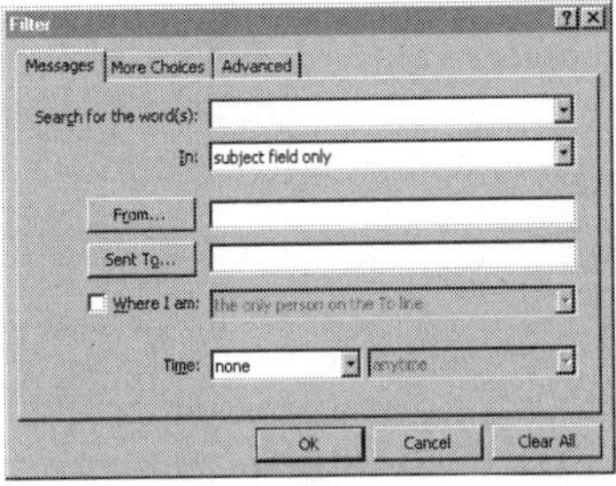

Filtering Messages by Sender

To filter messages by sender, first use the From box to specify the name of the sender whose messages you want to see. If you don't know the sender's **e-mail name,** click the From button to display the **Address Book** and use it to identify the sender. You can, by the way, specify more than one sender—all you need to do is separate their e-mail names with semicolons.

continues

Inbox Filters *(continued)*

Filtering Messages by Recipient

You can filter messages by **recipient,** too, although you wouldn't do this with the messages in your Inbox folder. (In your **Inbox,** you are the recipient.) To filter messages by recipient, use the Sent To box to specify the name of the recipient whose messages you want to see. If you don't know the recipient's e-mail name, click the Sent To button to display the Address Book and use it to identify the recipient. If you specify more than one recipient, separate their e-mail names with semicolons.

Check the Where I Am box, and click The Only Person On The To Line to see only those messages that name you specifically as the recipient (rather than name a **distribution list** on which your name appears). And click On The CC Line With Other People to see only those messages that are actually copies of messages sent to another recipient.

Filtering Messages by Subject and Text

You can filter messages on the basis of their **subjects** or the text in the **message body.** To filter messages in these ways, enter a snippet of text in the Search For The Word(s) box. Then, using the In box, tell Outlook whether to search for the word(s) you seek in the subject field only or in the subject field and message body.

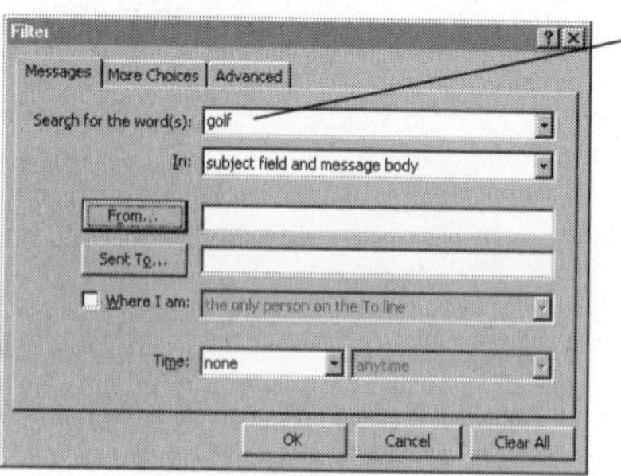

To see only messages that have something to do with golf, type the word *golf* in the Search For The Word(s) box.

Filtering Messages by Category

You can filter messages based on the **categories** you assigned them. Click the More Choices tab of the Filter dialog box. Click Categories, and then in the Available Categories list, click the message categories you want. Click OK twice to filter the information viewer by category.

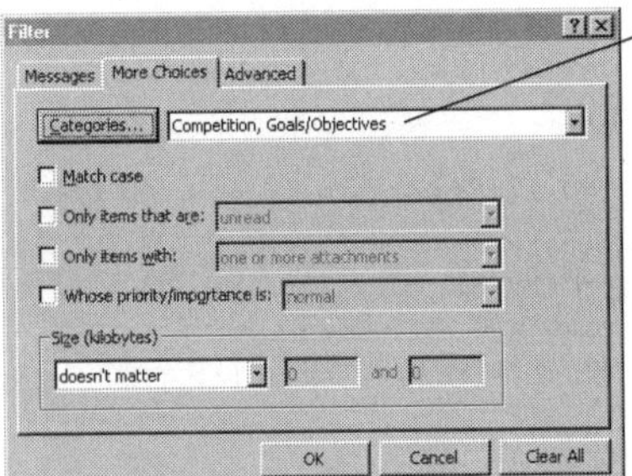

Choose one or more categories to narrow down a list of messages.

About the Clear All button and Advanced tab

The Filter dialog box provides numerous other choices—let me quickly describe two of them before you're off to some other entry or you get back to doing real work. You can click the Clear All button to remove any of the filters in the Filter dialog box. And you can click the Advanced tab to display boxes and buttons for filtering messages even more precisely.

Filters; Task Filters; Views

Information Service The **Outlook client** uses what are called information services to send and receive **e-mail,** pass information between the Outlook client and the Exchange server, and get address information from the server. Think of these services as features or capabilities of the Exchange Server software.

Information Store The Information Store is where all of your **messages** and everyone else's messages get stored. Since we're on this topic, I should mention that there are really two parts to the Information Store: the public Information Store and the private Information Store. The public Information Store holds messages stored in **public folders.** Anybody with permission can view a message in a public folder. The private Information Store holds messages stored in **private folders.** The stuff stored in a private folder is, well, private. Only the **sender** and **recipient** of a message can view it.

Information Viewer The term *information viewer* refers to the right half of the Outlook program window. The information viewer just shows the **items** stored in the selected **folder.**

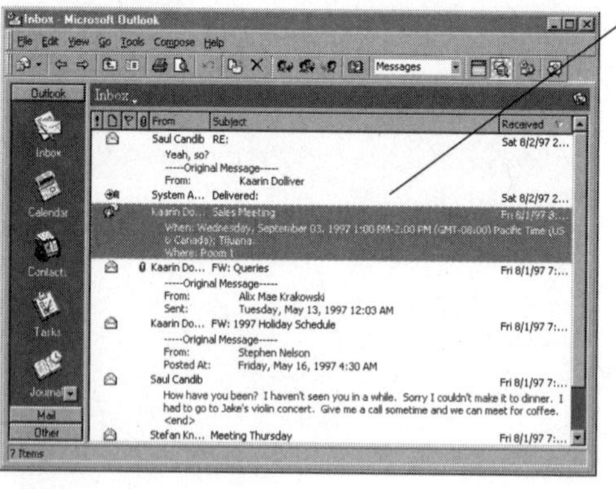

This is the information viewer.

Columns; Fields

Internet Once you understand that a **network** is just a bunch of computers that are connected so that information, including e-mail **messages,** can be shared, it's easy to understand what the Internet is: the Internet is a network of networks. The Internet may seem more appropriate as the topic of a U.S. Senate hearing or a story in a weekly news magazine, but it is important to Outlook users, too.

Why? Because if your **organization's** network is connected to the Internet, you can easily send e-mail to anybody else connected to the Internet: the President of the United States, Bill Gates, or Mick Jagger. (You do need to know the recipient's **e-mail name**, however.)

Hyperlink; URL; World Wide Web

Items

In Outlook, each **appointment, task, message, contact,** meeting, journal entry, or note is called an **item.** Even files and **folders** are considered to be items. You can act upon items in a variety of ways: for example, you can send, **sort, filter, group, forward,** print, **copy,** move, and delete items.

Item-Specific Menu

Outlook provides six different **Outlook Folders: Inbox, Calendar, Contacts, Tasks, Journal,** and **Notes,** which work like mini-applications. These six folders all use the same basic command menus with just one exception: each folder also provides a unique menu named after the **Outlook item** the folder works with.

For example, the Tasks folder provides the standard set of Outlook menus, but it also provides a Tasks menu. And the Contacts folder provides the standard set of Outlook menus, but it also provides a Contacts menu. I call these special menus item-specific menus to distinguish them from the File, Edit, View, Go, Tools, and other standard menus.

By the way, because the Outlook Folders use such similar menus, once you learn how to work with one folder, you'll find it very easy to work with the others.

Quick Reference: Item-Specific Menu Commands

Journal The Journal is an **Outlook Folder** that tracks the history of an activity and displays that history on a timeline. If the activity you want to track is an Outlook **item,** such as a phone call to a contact, you can record it automatically in the Journal. You can even use the Journal to record **Microsoft Word** documents, Microsoft Excel spreadsheets, and Microsoft Access databases that you create.

But even if you want to track an activity that has nothing whatever to do with Outlook, you can still use the Journal by adding entries to the Journal manually. So you could use the Journal to keep track of your off-track betting, for example. No, on second thought, forget that.

Journal entries appear as icons on the timeline. After you've recorded several activities, your Journal timeline appears something like the one shown below.

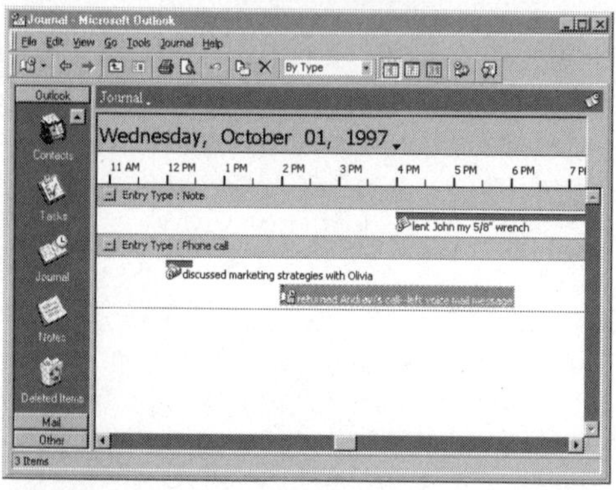

Using the Journal to Automatically Track Interactions with Contacts

Using the Journal, you can keep track of **e-mail** messages and faxes you send to and receive from selected **contacts**. You can also record meeting and task requests to and responses from your contacts.

To automatically record interactions with existing contacts, follow these steps:

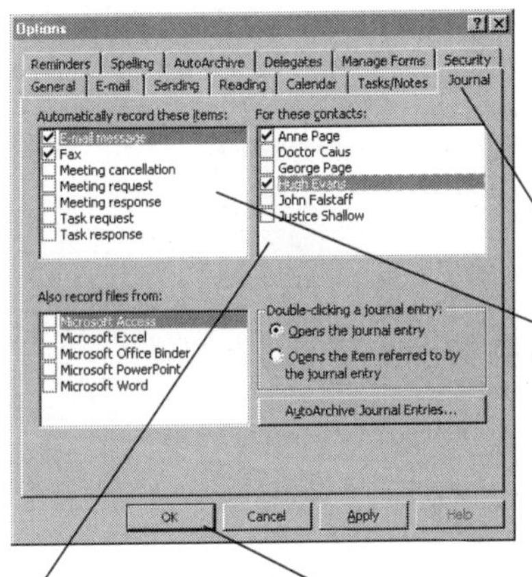

1 Choose Options from the Tools menu. Outlook displays the Options dialog box.

2 Click the Journal tab.

3 In the Automatically Record These Items box, check the items you want to automatically record in the Journal.

4 In the For These Contacts box, check the names of the contacts you want to record your interactions with.

5 Click OK. Outlook will make a Journal entry any time you interact in the indicated manner with any of the contacts you selected.

You can also elect to track contact activity when you add a new contact. When you fill out the New Contact form for the new contact, click the Journal tab.

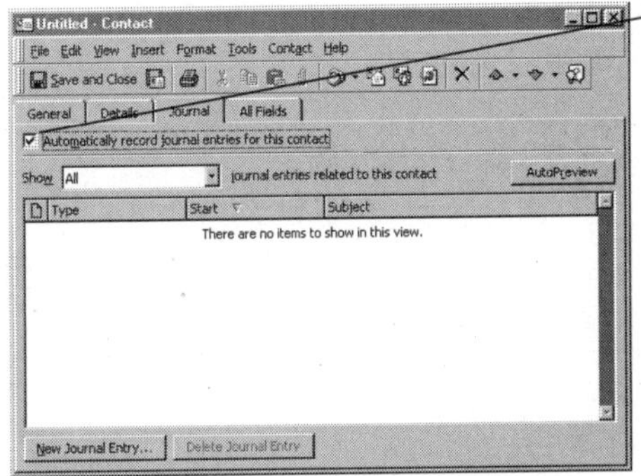

Check this box to automatically record journal entries for interactions with the new contact.

continues

Journal *(continued)*

Using the Journal to Record Documents You Create

To record any new files you create in other Microsoft Office 97 applications, check the names of the applications you want to track in the Also Record These Applications box of the Journal tab of the Tools menu Options dialog box.

Using the Journal to Record Phone Calls to Contacts

Whenever you call a contact using Outlook's **AutoDial** feature, you can make a record of the phone call. This could come in handy for billing a customer for time spent on the phone, for instance, or simply to jog your memory later.

To record a phone call to a contact, select the contact and click the AutoDialer toolbar button. Outlook displays the New Call dialog box.

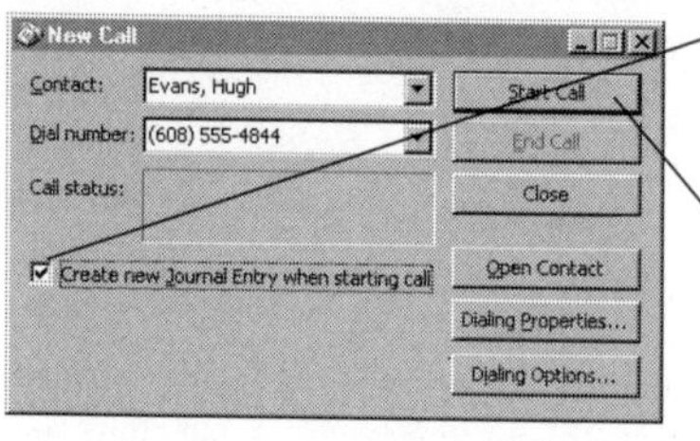

Click this box to record a Journal entry for a phone call.

Click Start Call, and Outlook displays the Start Call dialog box. Click Talk, pick up your phone, and Outlook displays the Phone Call form.

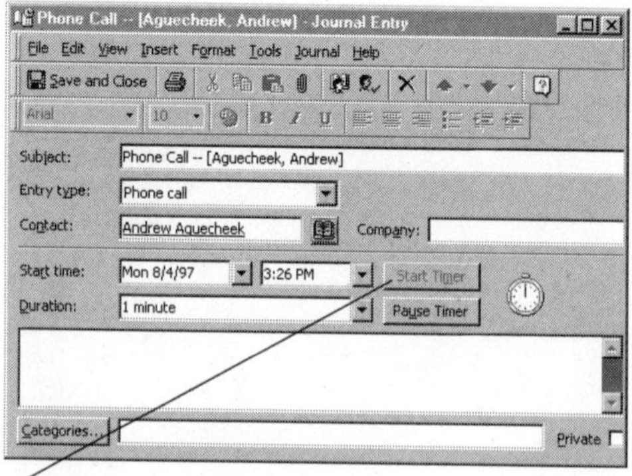

Click Start Timer to keep track of the length of the call. When the call is complete, click Pause Timer and click End Call. You can type notes about the call in the text area of the form either while the call is in progress or after you hang up. When you've finished writing notes, click Save and Close.

Manually Recording Outlook Items in the Journal

To manually record any Outlook item in the Journal, just open that item. To record a meeting, for example, display the Meeting form. Choose Record In Journal from the Tools menu. Outlook displays the Journal Entry form for the meeting.

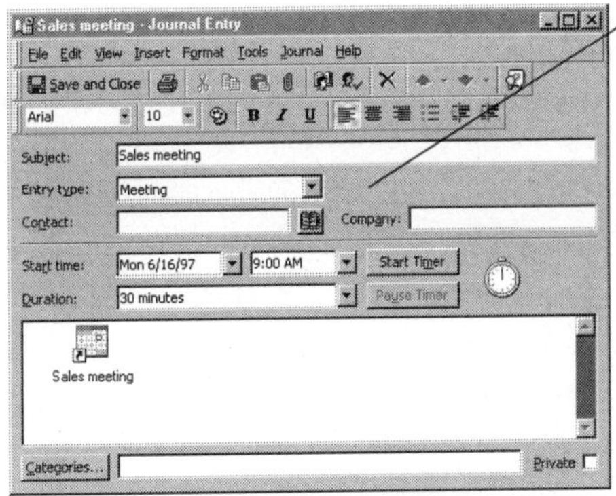

Fill in the text boxes to describe the meeting for the Journal Entry.

Manually Recording Miscellaneous Activities in the Journal

You can make a record of just about anything you want in the Journal. Click the arrow next to the New Item toolbar button to display the New Item drop-down list, and choose Journal Entry. Outlook displays the Untitled—Journal Entry form. Describe the entry type, and then fill out the rest of the boxes to describe the activity, event, or whatever. Then click Save And Close to record it in the Journal.

Contacts

Mailbox If you're using Outlook as part of a network, a mailbox is where your **messages** get stored. Messages you've received are stored in the Mailbox's **Inbox** folder. Messages you've sent are stored in the Mailbox's Sent Items folder. Messages you've sent that haven't yet been delivered to the **server** are stored in the Mailbox's Outbox folder. And, oh yes, there's another Mailbox folder called Deleted Items that stores messages you've deleted from the other Mailbox folders.

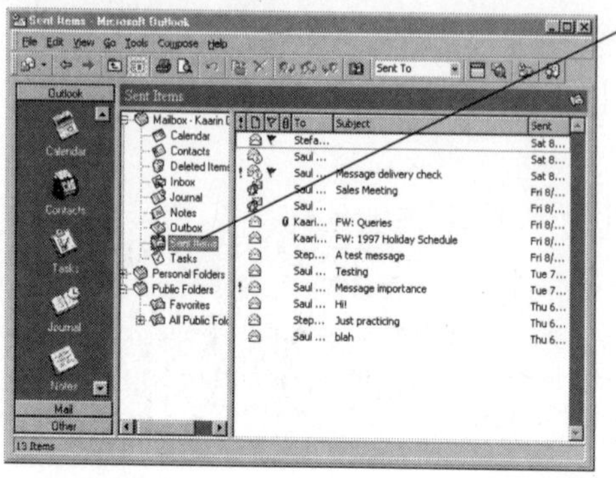

To see the messages in a folder, click its icon.

Mail Folders Mail folders include all the folders dealing with Outlook's **e-mail** functions—Inbox, Outbox, Sent Items, and Deleted Items. You can open a Mail folder by clicking its icon in the **Outlook Bar** or in the **Folder List**.

Meeting Planner Outlook's Meeting Planner is a nifty way to schedule meetings. When you choose Plan A Meeting from the **Calendar,** Compose (in the Inbox), or **Contacts** menus, Outlook displays the Plan A Meeting dialog box. Outlook checks your schedule and that of the other invitees and finds a time slot that appears as free time on everyone's schedule.

Planning a Meeting

To schedule a meeting from the Calendar folder, choose Plan A Meeting from the Calendar menu. Outlook displays the Plan A Meeting dialog box. Your name appears on the first line of the All Attendees list. Choose the day of the meeting by clicking a date in the Meeting Start Time drop-down calendar. Pick a tentative meeting time by dragging the green and red meeting selection bars.

Click here and type a name to add an invitee, or else click the Invite Others button and select names of invitees from your Address Book.

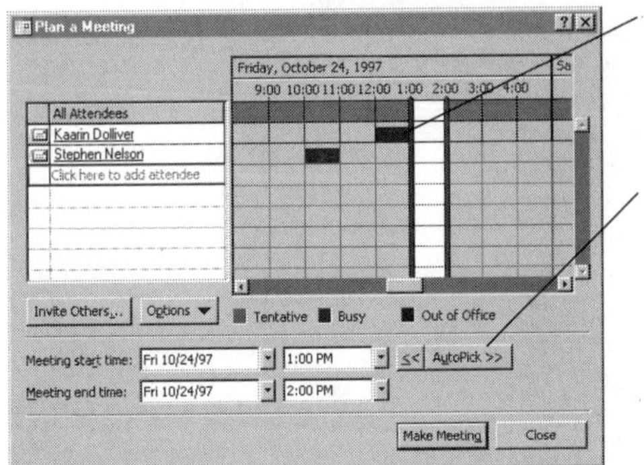

Busy times show up in blue on this schedule.

Click the AutoPick button to find the next available time slot that's free for all attendees.

Click Make Meeting to add the meeting to your Calendar and to send invitations to the other prospective attendees.

Megabyte As you may already know, a byte is an 8-digit string of 1s and 0s that your computer uses to represent a character. A kilobyte is roughly 1000 of these bytes. (Or to be precise, a kilobyte is exactly 1024 of these bytes.) A megabyte is roughly 1 million of these bytes. (Or, again, to be absolutely precise, a megabyte is 1,048,576 bytes. Oh my.)

Message Messages are the communiqués you pass around with Outlook. The joke you send to your boss. The birthday greeting to a friend who works on the other side of the country. The electronic letter you send to everyone in the sales department. What makes Outlook special is that it artfully handles all of these items for you.

Writing a Message

To write a message, if you're already in the Inbox, click the New Mail Message button. Otherwise, click the down-arrow next to the New Item button (the button changes depending upon which Outlook module you're in) to display the New Item menu, and choose Mail Message. Outlook displays the **Message form.** If you use the default Outlook e-mail text editor, your Message form looks pretty much like the one shown in this figure.

1 Enter the **e-mail name** of the **recipient**.

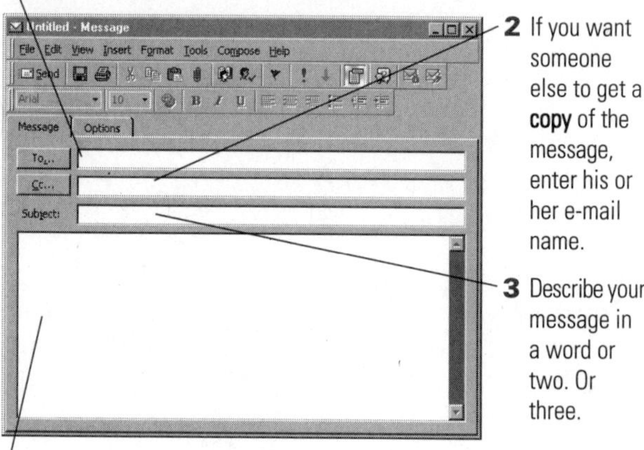

2 If you want someone else to get a **copy** of the message, enter his or her e-mail name.

3 Describe your message in a word or two. Or three.

4 Type your message text here.

Click the Options tab to set general message options (such as **Importance**) and other delivery and tracking options.

Attaching a File to a Message

Many messages only include text typed into the Message form. But you can also **attach** a **file** to a message. In this way, you can include in your e-mail items such as word-processed documents, spreadsheets, and anything else you can store as a file on your hard disk. To attach a file, click the Insert File toolbar button. When Outlook displays the Insert File dialog box, use its boxes to name the file and identify its disk location.

Use the Look In box to identify the file's disk location.

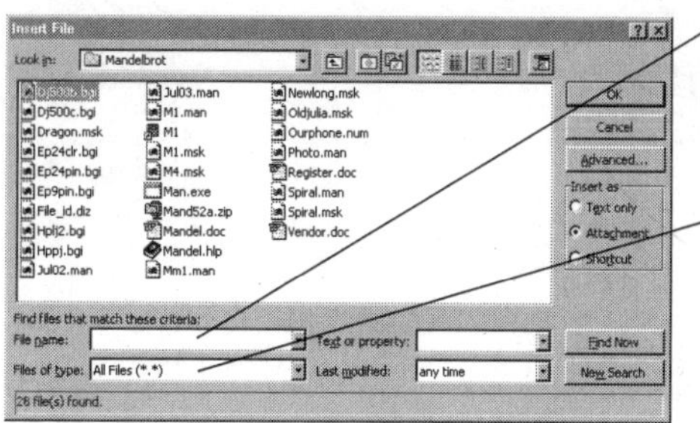

Use the File Name box to give the file's name.

Use the Files Of Type list box to specify which types of files you want to see listed in the Insert File dialog box.

You have a choice

You get a choice as to the way Outlook attaches the file to your message. If your file is a text file and you just want to plug the text into your message, click Insert As Text Only (which tells Outlook to insert the file as a text file into your message—something you would typically do only with text files). If your file isn't just a bunch of text, click either Insert As Attachment or Insert As Shortcut. Clicking Insert As Attachment tells Outlook to stick an actual copy of the file into the message. The Insert As Shortcut option inserts into your message a shortcut icon that merely points to a file on a computer. When Outlook later sends the message, it uses this shortcut to find the file with the actual message. (The recipient must have access to the location at which the file is stored.)

continues

Message *(continued)*

Attaching Other Items to Your Message

You can attach any existing Outlook item to your message. In other words, you can insert other messages, **Calendar** files, **Contact list** items, **Notes**, and so forth. To do this, choose Item from the Insert menu to display the Insert Item dialog box. Use the Insert Item dialog box to identify the item you want to send and tell Outlook how you want it inserted.

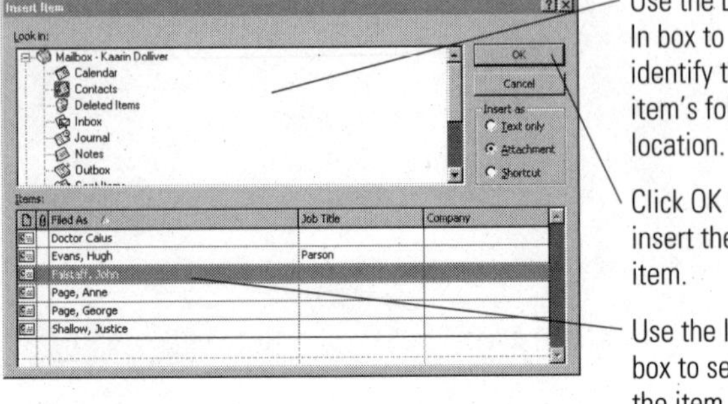

Attaching Objects to a Message

You can attach **OLE** objects to a message. You do this in the same way that you insert an OLE object in any document. Just choose Object from the Insert menu. For specific instructions on inserting objects, refer to the **Embedding and Linking Existing Objects** and **Embedding New Objects** entries in this book.

Sending a Message

After you write a message, send it by clicking the Send button. Outlook sends your message to the recipient you named. In a few minutes—maybe sooner—he or she receives the message. But it's anybody's guess how long it will be before the recipient reads it.

Reading Your Messages

To read the messages that other people have sent you, display the **Inbox** folder by clicking its icon in the Outlook window or **Outlook Bar**. Outlook lists any messages you've received. Unread messages are displayed in boldface. To view a message, double-click it. When you do this, Outlook displays the message in its own window.

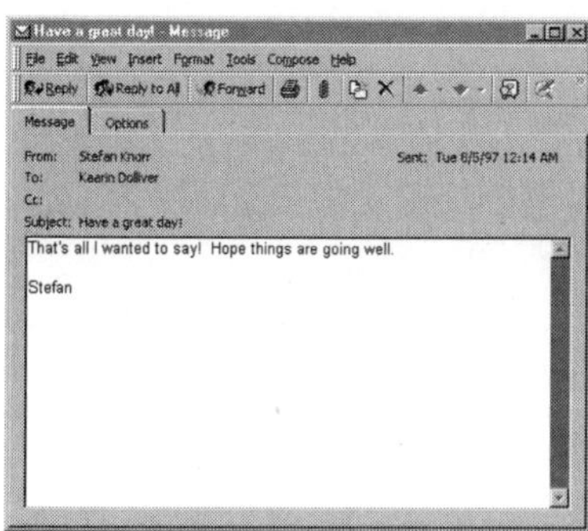

When you get done reading a message, you can simply close the window. This tells Outlook to save the message in your Inbox folder and not do anything else with it. Alternatively, you can click the Delete toolbar button. This tells Outlook to move the message to the Deleted Items folder. (Presumably, you move messages to the Deleted Items folder as a last stop before you zap them forever by choosing Empty "Deleted Items" Folder from the Tools menu.)

Replying to a Message

It's easy to reply to messages that others have sent you. To do this, click either the Reply or the Reply To All toolbar buttons. The Reply To Sender button tells Outlook you want to send a message only to the person who originally sent the message to you. The Reply To All button tells Outlook that you want to send a message to the original sender and to everyone else who received a copy of the message. After you click either the Reply or the Reply To All buttons, Outlook opens a new Message form that holds a copy of the original message and correctly names the recipients to whom you want to send the message. You type in your reply and click the Send button.

continues

Message *(continued)*

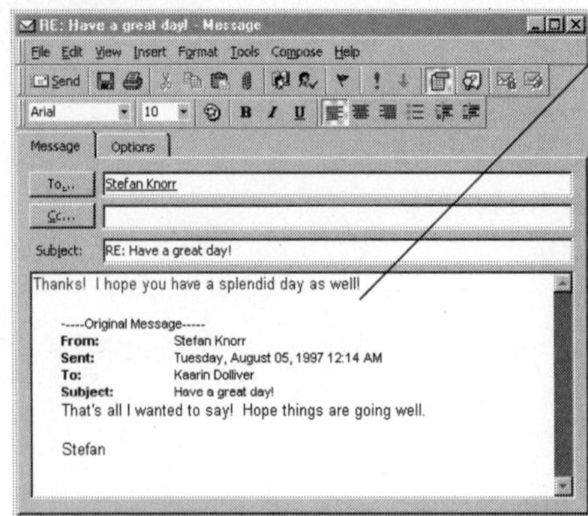

Whatever you type in your reply message gets inserted here.

Forwarding a Message

It's just as easy to forward a message you received from someone else. First either select the message in the Outlook window by clicking it or display the message in its form. Next click the Forward toolbar button. After you click the Forward button, Outlook opens a new Message form that holds a copy of the original message.

Specify to whom you want to forward the message by entering the e-mail name. (Click the To button to open your **Address Book.**)

Add comments to the message by typing some more stuff in here.

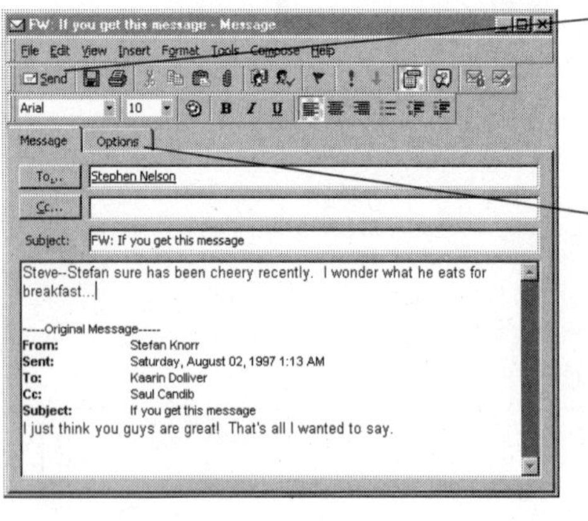

Click the Send button when you want to send the message.

Click the Options tab to set general message options (such as **Importance**) and other delivery and tracking options.

Printing a Message

You can print the messages you write and receive. To do this, just select the message and click the Print button.

If you want more control over how your message is printed, you can choose Print from the File menu. When you choose this command, Outlook displays the Print dialog box. You can use it to choose a printer, tell Outlook how many copies to print, describe what Outlook should do about any attachments, and so forth.

Use the Name box to select the printer.

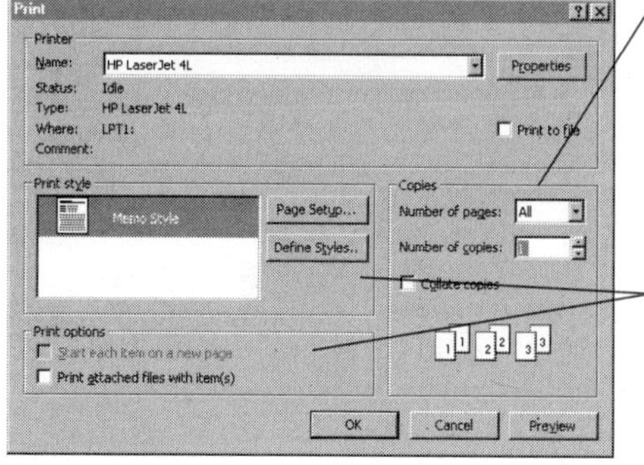

Use the Copies box to tell Outlook to print more than one copy of the message.

Use these boxes and buttons to set printing style and other printing options.

Message Body The message body is the actual message. In other words, it's the text element of the message, not the **e-mail name** of the **sender** or the **recipient**, or the message **subject**.

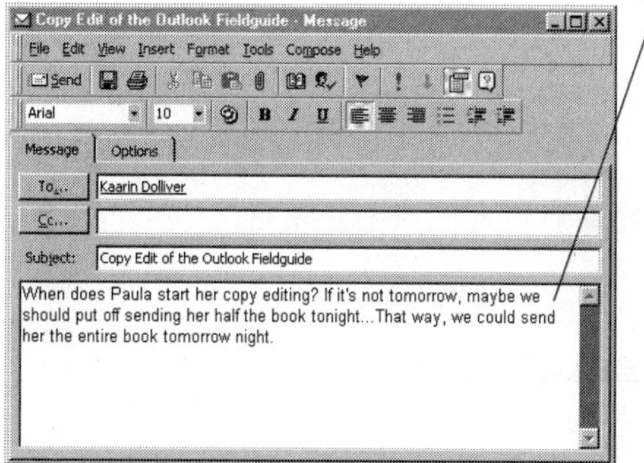

This chunk of text is the message body.

Message Box A message box is simply a miniature dialog box that displays a message from a Windows-based application. It also usually displays some command buttons, such as OK and Cancel.

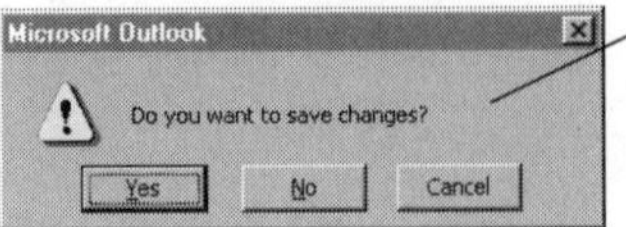

This is the message box that Outlook displays if you try to close a message that has unsaved changes. Rather than OK and Cancel, it uses Yes, No, and Cancel command buttons.

Message Flag When you flag a message, you mark it with a flag icon, either to remind yourself to take further action or to ask someone else to act. Message flags appear in two places: as a message bar added to the **Message form** itself and in the Flag Status **column** of the Message view of the **Inbox information viewer.**

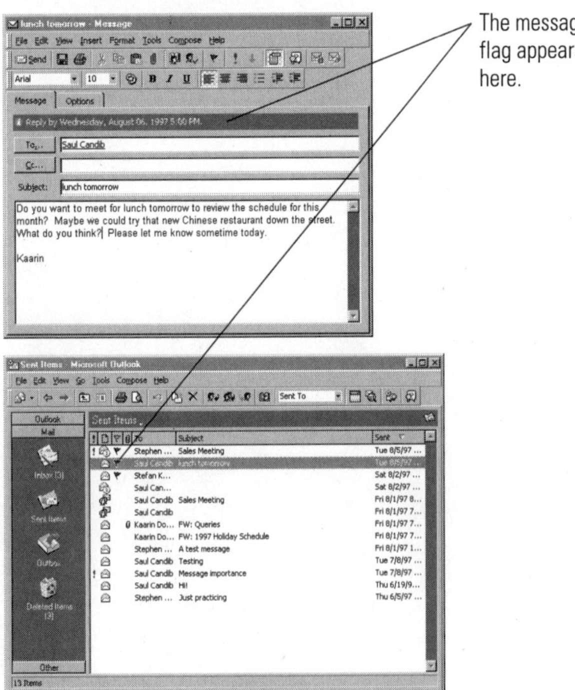

The message flag appears here.

Message flags come in several different flavors. You can add one of the following flags to a message: Call, Follow Up, Forward, Read, Reply, Reply To All, or Review. Or you can invent a message flag of your own. You can also set a due date by which you want the suggested action taken.

Flagging a Message

To flag a message, open an existing message form or click New Message. Click the Message Flag button on the toolbar. Outlook displays the Flag Message dialog box.

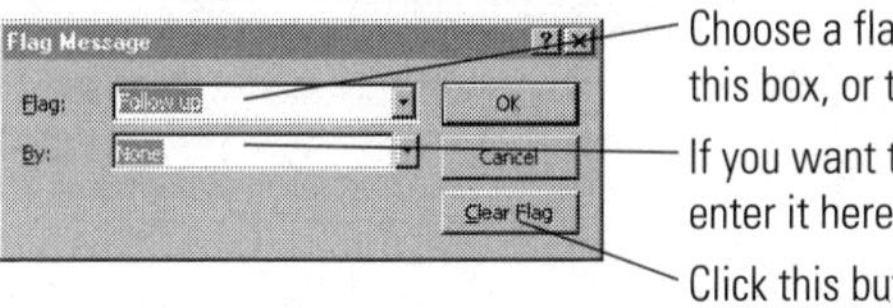

Flagged messages to which responses are overdue appear in red in the information viewer.

Message Form The Message form is the window that Outlook displays so you can write **e-mail messages.** Why it's called a **form** instead of a window is sometimes confusing. But all you need to understand to keep from getting confused is that Outlook calls the windows you use to collect information—such as an e-mail message—forms. In the case of an e-mail message, "form" doesn't fit the bill very well. For the **custom forms** that Outlook lets you create, however, "form" works quite nicely. You can create forms, for example, for reporting employee business expenses. (In this case, employees would fill out business expense forms and e-mail them to Mildred in accounts payable.)

continues

Message Form *(continued)*

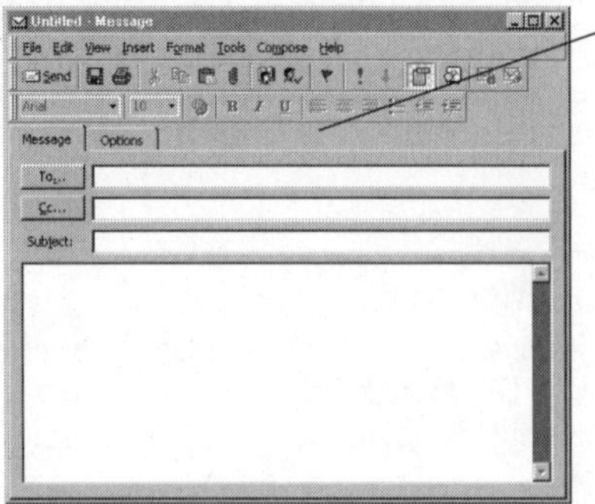

This is the Message form. You can also call it the Message form window.

Message Header

The message header lists the **sender, recipient,** message **subject,** and a bunch of other information. All you really need to know about the message header is this: if you right-click different parts of the message header, such as the sender name, you access a shortcut menu of commands that you can use to do neat things.

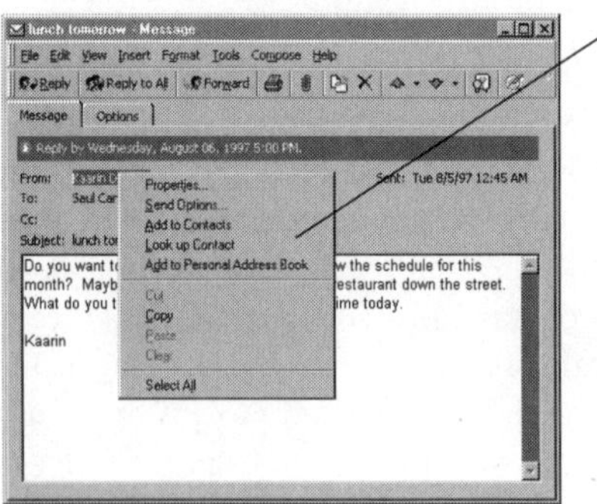

When you right-click one of the recipient names in the message header, Outlook displays a shortcut menu with a command for adding the person to your **Contacts folder.**

Message Options

You can set various options for the **e-mail messages** you send. These options fall into three categories: General options, Delivery options, and Tracking options. I discuss many of these options individually elsewhere in this book.

You can set message options for all your messages at one fell swoop. The way you do that is to click the Sending tab of the Options dialog box, which you display by choosing Options from the Tools menu.

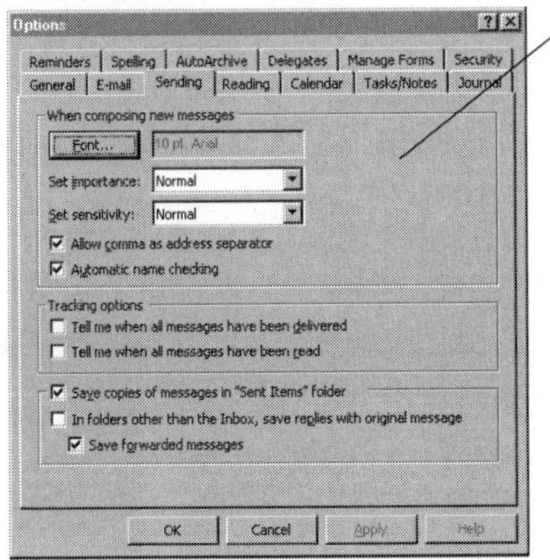

You can set options that will apply to all your e-mail messages on this Options dialog box tab.

Or you can set options individually for each message as you write it. Just click the Options tab of the New Message form whenever you're about to send a message. Incidentally, if you've set mail options in the Options dialog box, the settings you make for individual messages override the general ones.

Delivery Receipt; Importance; Read Receipt; Sensitivity

Message Subject Subject

Microsoft Word Microsoft Word is Microsoft's best-selling word-processing program. But I didn't include this entry to plug the program. (I'm pretty sure Microsoft can sell a lot of copies without my help.) I mention it because if you have Word 7.0 or a later version and you're running Windows 95, or if you have Word 6.0 and you're running Windows 3.x or Windows NT, you can use Word as your e-mail editor. (But you do need to tell the Word Setup program you want to make this option available when you install Word.) In other words, when you write those cogent **messages** of yours, you can call on the power of Word to assist you.

continues

Microsoft Word *(continued)*

To use Word as an e-mail editor, choose Options from the Tools menu. When Outlook displays the Options dialog box, click the Mail tab. Then click to check the Use Microsoft Word As E-Mail Editor box.

You may not want to use WordMail

Using **WordMail** as your e-mail editor seems like a good idea. And usually it is. But you may not want to use it if you often run the regular Word program at the same time as you compose new messages with WordMail. The Word program uses up a lot of computer memory. And if you use both Word and WordMail (which is really like a second copy of Word), your computer's responsiveness slows down, sometimes drastically.

Smiley

MIME

MIME stands for "multipurpose **Internet** mail extensions." MIME is a protocol that lets you attach binary **files** to **e-mail** messages and send these over the Internet. As long as the people you send messages to also have e-mail readers that support the MIME protocol, they can extract and use the files you send them. For example, using MIME, someone can stick a Microsoft Word for Windows document in an e-mail message. If the recipient's e-mail reader supports MIME, the recipient can extract the Word document from the e-mail message. If the recipient has a copy of Word for Windows, he or she can open and work with the document in Word.

While Outlook understands and supports the MIME protocol, not all e-mail systems do. For this reason, sometimes you can't use MIME. Sometimes you need to use **Uuencode.**

Network A network is just a bunch of computers that are hooked together so that the people who use the computers can share information. If you're using Outlook to send e-mail to co-workers, by the way, your computer is connected to a network.

Notes Notes is one of the **Outlook Folders,** and notes themselves are just like, well, electronic sticky notes. (I think you know the brand name I'm referring to.) You can use an Outlook note to write down a phone number, an address, a quick to-do list—all the things you put on paper notes. As you can with the paper kind, you can stick one of these notes on your desktop where it will serve as a reminder to you—until you get around to filing it more permanently or tossing it in the trash.

Writing a Note

Writing a note is simplicity itself. Just click Note on the New Object drop-down list, and a blank Note pops up on your screen, already marked with the date and time. Type whatever it is you want to make note of, and you've created a Note.

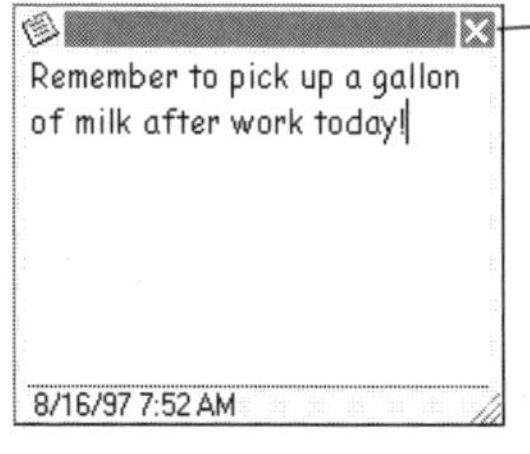

Click the X to close a Note and add it to the Notes list.

Customizing a Note

Click the icon in the Note's upper left corner to display the Note's Control menu. Click Color to change the Note's color. Click **Categories** to assign the Note to a category. Whenever you use the Taskbar to switch to another application, you always minimize any visible Notes. If you close or minimize all other applications, you can leave a Note on your desktop so you'll see it the next time you glance at your screen.

continues

Notes *(continued)*

Once you type something on a Note, you enable the Cut and Copy commands on the Control menu. Then you can paste part or all of the Note into a message or wherever else you want. You can paste the clipboard's contents into a Note by choosing the Paste command from the Control menu.

Moving and Resizing a Note

You can resize a note by clicking and dragging its edges as you would with any other object. Or right-click the Note and use the Minimize and Maximize commands on the shortcut menu. Click and drag the Note's top bar (it's really not a title bar) to move it anywhere on the screen.

Keeping Track of Notes

To print a Note, just choose Print from the Control menu. To forward a Note, choose the **Forward** command. Outlook will open a Forward **Message form** that will let you send the Note anywhere you can send **e-mail**.

When you close a Note, it automatically gets posted to the Notes **information viewer**. To view the Notes information viewer, click Notes in the **Outlook Bar** or in the **Folder List**. You can **group** Notes as you would any other Outlook items. You can define **views** for the Notes list and use all the other information viewer features such as **sorting, filtering,** and **AutoPreview.**

Click Save As from the Control menu to save a Note to a folder anywhere on your hard disk.

Deleting a Note

To delete a note, select it in the Notes list and click the Delete button.

Color-coding your notes

By changing the color of Notes, you can code them. Make all your phone number Notes yellow and all your reminders blue. Or use whatever combination you like.

Office Assistant Microsoft Outlook Help is now supplied by the Office Assistant, an animated character that pops up whenever you click the Help button or choose Microsoft Outlook Help from the Help menu. When the Assistant appears, type a question and click Search. The Assistant will display the Help topics that most closely relate to your question. Or click Tips, and the Assistant will display a series of Tips that help you get the most out of Outlook.

You can customize the Office Assistant to suit your preferences using the Office Assistant dialog box.

Choosing an Assistant

To pick the particular Assistant you like, right-click the Assistant and choose the Choose Assistant command from the shortcut menu. You can pick an Assistant from a gallery of available characters on the Gallery tab of the Office Assistant dialog box. Your choices range from a paper clip to a robot to William Shakespeare and Albert Einstein look-alikes.

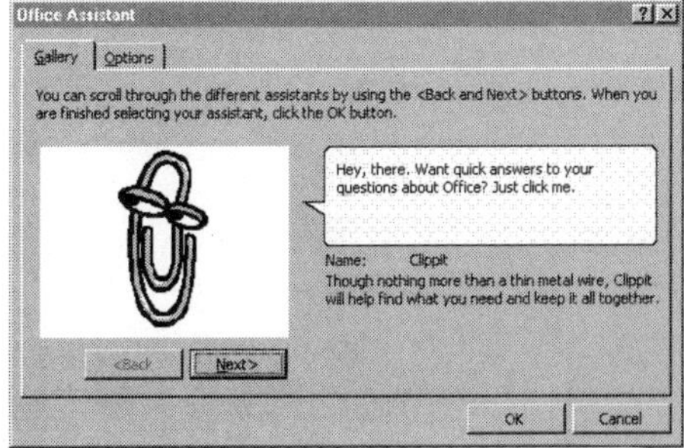

continues

Office Assistant *(continued)*

Setting Assistant Options

By choosing Options from the shortcut menu, you display the Options tab of the Office Assistant dialog box, where you can set a variety of options relating to the Assistant's capabilities. You can also set options that control how Tips are displayed.

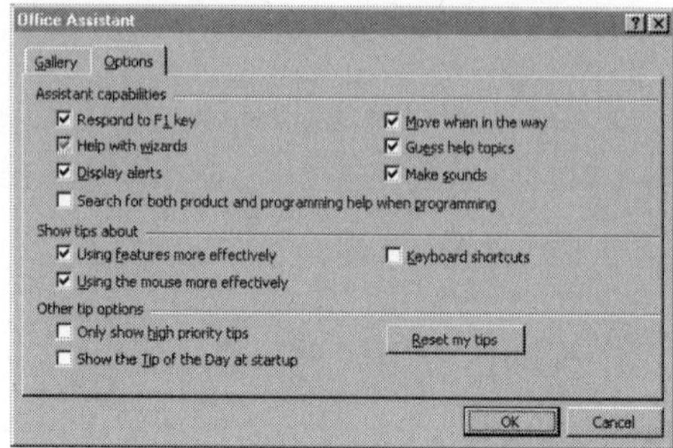

Hiding the Assistant

If the little bugger starts to drive you crazy, you can make it go away until you need it. Just choose Hide Assistant from the shortcut menu, or, click the Assistant's Close button and say, "¡Hasta la vista!"

Help

Offline Folders An offline folder is a copy of the server folder that Outlook uses to actually deliver and store **messages.** If you use an offline folder—say you're not currently connected to the **network**—you periodically need to get it updated by **synchronizing** your files. First, however, you'll need to reconnect to the network.

Remote Mail

OLE

OLE (object linking and embedding) is an integral part of Windows 95. You use it to create a compound document—a document **file** that includes two or more types of information. For example, you can create a compound **message** document that includes a Microsoft Excel worksheet and, a little while later, a drawing created with Microsoft Word's drawing tools. In this case, the compound message document really consists of stuff created in different **programs** and pasted together into one big compound document (which just happens to be a message).

Let me tell you one other thing about OLE. Perhaps the most important tidbit for you to know is that OLE is very easy to use. You don't have to do anything other than copy and paste the things—called objects—that you want to plop into the compound document.

Using OLE to Create Compound Documents

To do all this pasting together, you can often use the application's Copy and Paste (or Paste Special) commands, usually found on the Edit menu, or often as toolbar buttons. If you're creating a compound document in Outlook, you can click Object on the Insert menu.

Distinguishing Between Linked Objects and Embedded Objects

OLE enables you to link or embed objects. A linked object—remember, it could be an Excel worksheet you've pasted into a message—gets updated whenever the source document changes. An embedded object doesn't. You can, however, double-click an embedded object to open the program with which the embedded object was created so that you can make your changes.

Embedding and Linking Existing Objects; Embedding New Objects

Online Service You can use the Outlook **client** to send and receive **e-mail** over an online service such as The Microsoft Network (MSN) or CompuServe. To do this, however, you'll need to have your **administrator** describe to Outlook how these connections are supposed to work.

Organization Outlook uses the term *organization* a lot, especially in its online documentation, so it makes sense to understand what the term means. According to Outlook, an organization is a bunch of Exchange **servers** and Outlook **clients** that work happily together. In a little company, the organization might consist of a single server and half a dozen clients. In a big company, the organization might consist of dozens of servers and hundreds of clients scattered across multiple sites.

Other Folders Folder icons in the **Outlook Bar** are divided into three sections: Outlook folders, Mail folders, and Other folders. Outlook folders include the various **Outlook item** folders— **Inbox, Calendar, Contacts, Tasks, Journal,** and **Notes,** along with Deleted Items. Mail folders include all the folders dealing with Outlook's e-mail functions—Inbox, Outbox, Sent Items, and Deleted Items.

Other folders include **public folders,** which are like Outlook folders, but are open to public view because they are shared on your local network. In addition, Other folders include three familiar friends from Windows —My Computer, My Documents, and Favorites. Using these folders from within Outlook, you can open files and launch programs anywhere on your computer, your local network, or on the **World Wide Web,** just possibly making Outlook the only interface you really ever need.

Favorites

The Favorites folder is a subfolder of the Windows folder. It's the repository of all the **World Wide Web** site addresses (**URL**s) you tell your browser to remember. In addition, you can add folders and files to Favorites using the Add To Favorites toolbar button found in the Open dialog box of many Windows programs, including all the Office applications.

Because it's so easy to place your favorite files, folders, and Web site addresses in Favorites, it's really pretty convenient to have a shortcut to Favorites in the Outlook Bar.

My Computer

You use My Computer to navigate the folders, files, and features of your computer. My Computer is simply a picture of your computer and its contents, both hardware and software. When you click the My Computer icon in the Outlook Bar, you see other icons that represent the various parts of your computer. You can then double-click any of those icons to get information about or use that particular part.

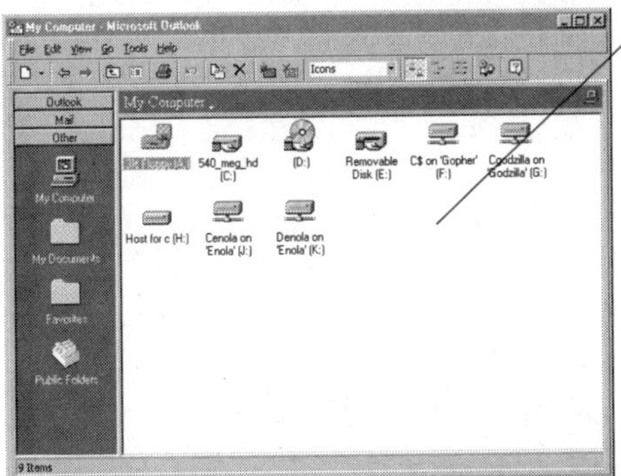

The My Computer window is like a picture of your computer.

My Documents

My Documents is a folder on your hard drive that, by default, is where the Save dialog box sends Office files to be saved and where the Open dialog box looks for Office files you want to open. It's possible to change the default and save files to other folders. But the My Documents folder works just fine for me. I create subfolders in My Documents so that I can file all the documents I create where they belong. It's handy to have My Documents in the Outlook Bar.

continues

Other Folders *(continued)*

Public Folders

If you're part of a network, you'll have a Public Folders icon on your Outlook Bar. I explain public folders under their own entry, so I won't say any more about them here.

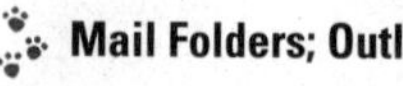
Mail Folders; Outlook Folders

Outlook Bar

The Outlook Bar lets you move around not only among the various Outlook folders but around your entire computer and even your local network. You can use the Outlook Bar in place of the Outlook **Folder List** to cruise around Outlook; furthermore, you can use it like Windows Explorer or My Computer to access any folder on your hard drive, other network drives, or on the Internet. And if there's a folder or **Web page** you find yourself accessing frequently, you can place a shortcut to it on the Outlook Bar.

Using the Outlook Bar to Navigate Around Outlook

When you open Outlook, you see the **Inbox**. To move to another Outlook folder, click its icon in the Outlook Bar.

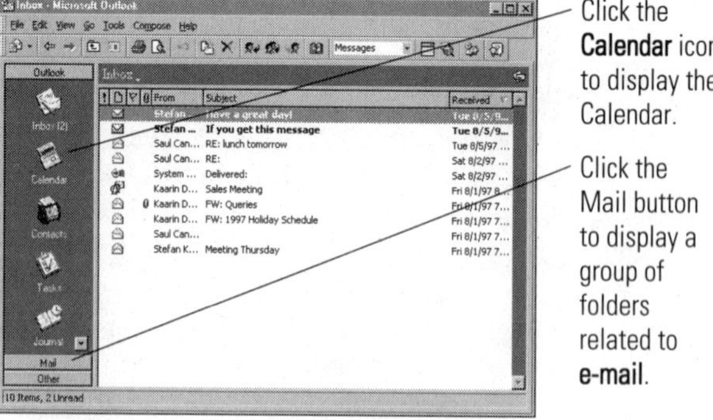

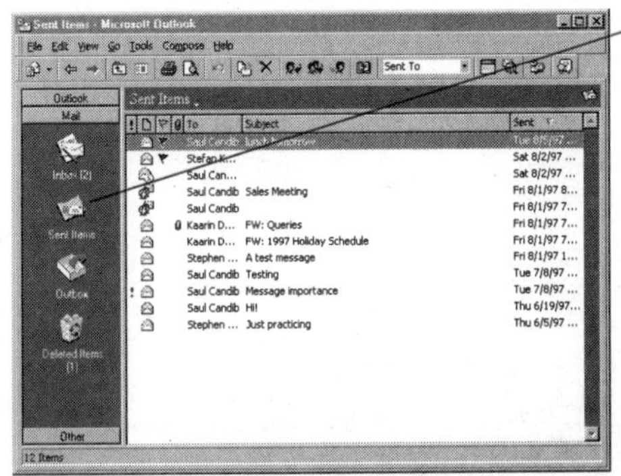
Click the Sent Items icon to display all the e-mail items you've sent recently.

Accessing My Computer, Other Folders, and the Internet Using the Outlook Bar

Click the Other button to display the My Computer icon and the **Favorites** folder icons.

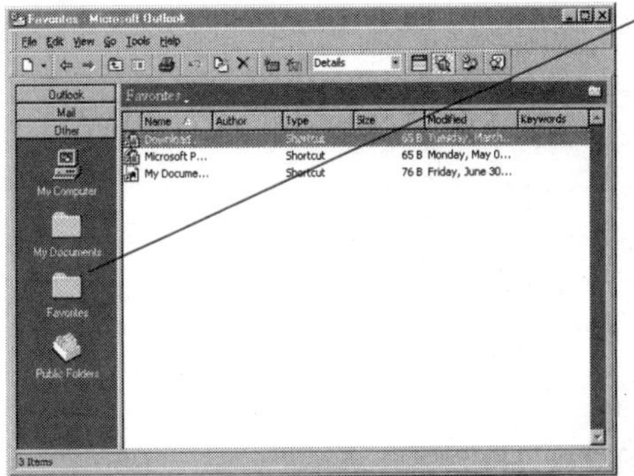
Click the Favorites icon to display the contents of the Favorites folder.

The Favorites folder contains the Internet addresses you've selected as your favorites while browsing the **World Wide Web**. Just click an icon to launch your **Web browser** and the Web page you picked.

continues

Outlook Bar *(continued)*

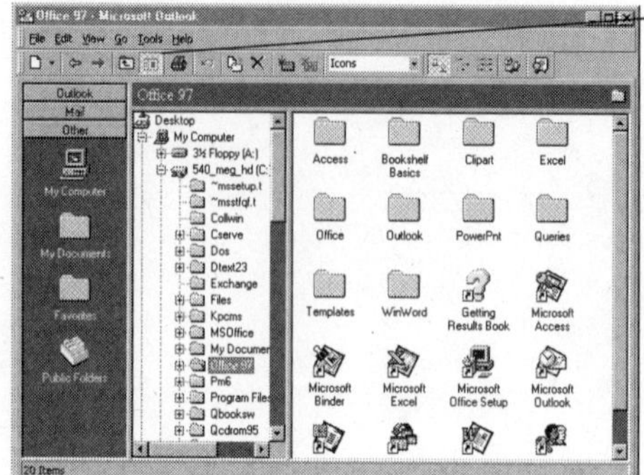

Click this button in the Folder List title bar to display a Windows Explorer-like folder hierarchy tree.

Taking a different view

Use the Current View box on the toolbar to switch the way you view the folder list in My Computer, My Documents, and Favorites. For example, to view folders as icons instead of as a detailed list, display the Current View box's drop-down list and choose Icons. Then click either the Large Icons or the Small Icons toolbar button.

Customizing the Outlook Bar

Want to add a shortcut to your favorite folder to the Outlook Bar? No problem. Follow these steps:

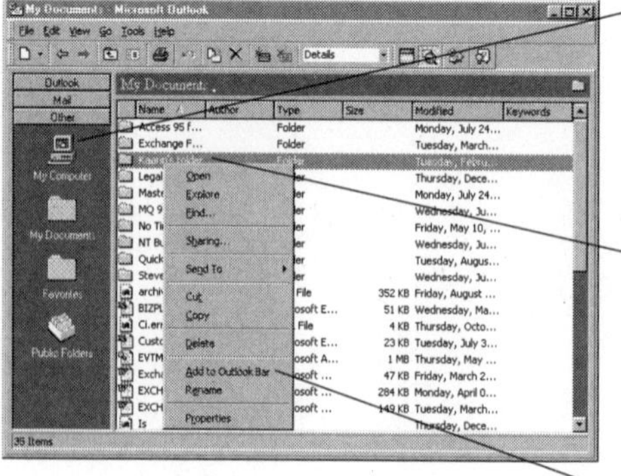

Click My Computer in the Outlook Bar to display the folder hierarchy.

Right-click the folder to which you want to create a shortcut.

Choose Add To Outlook Bar from the shortcut menu.

What's the big deal?

Why do I make such a fuss over the Outlook Bar? Why not just use Windows Explorer to navigate the folder hierarchy? Well, sure, there's nothing wrong with Windows Explorer. It's just that, if you're using Outlook to send and receive e-mail, check your schedule, and keep track of your contacts, you'll probably be spending a lot of time there. So why go to the trouble of minimizing Outlook and negotiating Windows Explorer or the Start menu when you can open files, launch programs, browse your network environment, and share files with other users right from within Outlook? It's simply a matter of convenience. I think you'll agree, anything that makes life a little easier is cool.

Outlook Client The Outlook messaging system really consists of two components: the Outlook client and the Exchange **server.** The Outlook client is a program that runs on your computer; the Exchange Server program runs on another computer. This Field Guide doesn't examine the server component of the Outlook messaging system except in passing. The server component of Outlook is the concern of the network **administrator.**

Outlook Folders This group of **folders** includes the Outlook Item folders: **Inbox, Calendar, Contacts, Tasks, Journal,** and **Notes.** You can open an Outlook folder by clicking its icon on the **Outlook Bar** or in the **Folder List.**

Mail Folders; Other Folders

Outlook Item **Item**

Out Of Office Assistant If you are using Outlook as a client for an Exchange server, you can use Outlook's Out Of Office Assistant to automatically reply to **messages** that people send. In this way, you can let people know, for example, that you're on vacation for two weeks. Or you can let people know that you are in meetings all day and cannot respond to messages in a timely manner.

Creating a Standard Response

To create a standard response that the Out Of Office Assistant can use to reply to every message you receive, choose Out Of Office Assistant from the Tools menu. Outlook displays the Out Of Office Assistant dialog box.

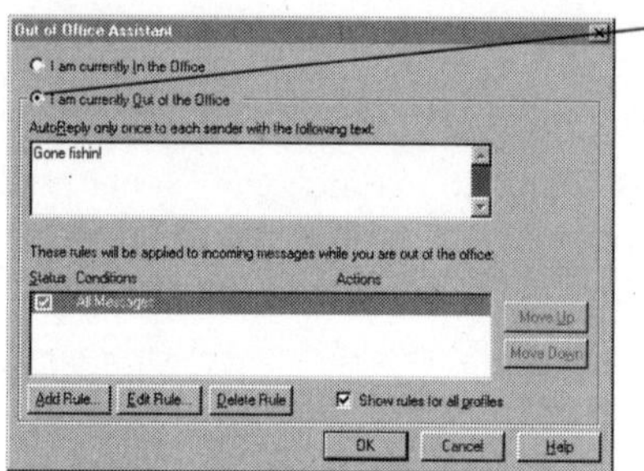

Click here to indicate that you're either out of your office or away from your computer.

Type a standard response that the Out Of Office Assistant can use to reply to all messages that arrive while you're away.

Using Rules and Actions

You may not want to handle all the incoming messages you receive when out of the office in the same way. If you want to be more specific, you can define rules that tell the Out Of Office Assistant how to monitor incoming messages and what to do when it sees a message you want processed in a certain way. To define rules such as these, choose Out Of Office Assistant from the Tools menu and click the Add Rule button. Outlook displays the Edit Rule dialog box. Use the When A Message Arrives That Meets The Following Conditions boxes and buttons to describe the rules. I need to point out, however, a tremendously important aspect of rules: a message must match *all* of the rules you specify before the Out Of Office Assistant can take action.

Enter the **sender** name or **recipient** name whose messages you want the Out Of Office Assistant to look for, using semicolons to separate multiple names. Then click the Check Names button to verify the spelling of the names.

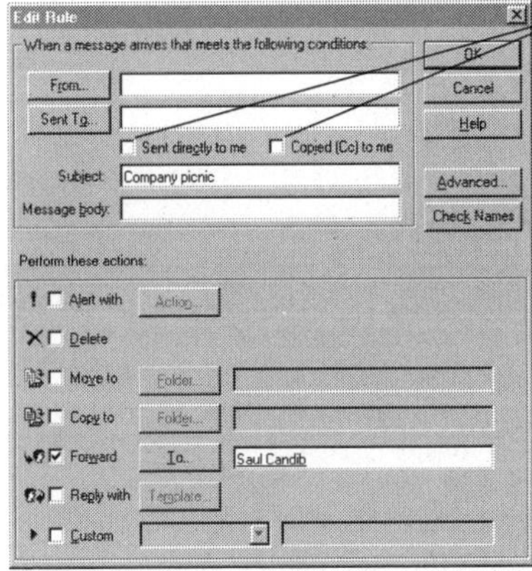

Use the Sent Directly To Me and Copied (Cc) To Me check boxes to tell the Out Of Office Assistant to look for messages sent directly to you or only copied to you.

Use the Subject and Message Body boxes to tell the Out Of Office Assistant to look for messages that include specific words or phrases, using semicolons to separate words or phrases. Here, for example, I'm looking for messages relating to the upcoming company picnic. (I'll tell Outlook to forward those messages to Saul.)

About the Advanced options

You can establish additional rules by clicking the Advanced button and using the Advanced dialog box's options. Its options let you tell the Out Of Office Assistant to look for messages with **attachments,** messages of a certain size, and messages that *don't* meet conditions you specify. (Usually the Out Of Office Assistant looks for messages that meet the conditions you specify.)

continues

Out Of Office Assistant *(continued)*

Describing Actions for the Out Of Office Assistant

After you define the rules for monitoring your incoming messages, you tell the Inbox Assistant what actions to take when it finds a message that meets the conditions described by your rules. To describe these rules, you use the Edit Rule dialog box's Perform These Actions options, which are described in the table that follows:

Action	Description
Alert With	Out Of Office Assistant displays a pop-up message (with text you supply) or makes a sound. (Specify whether you want the pop-up message or the sound by clicking the Action button.)
Delete	Moves the message to your Deleted Items folder.
Move To	Moves the message to another **folder.** (Specify the folder by clicking the Folder button beside this option.)
Copy To	Makes a copy of the message and places it in another folder. (Specify this other folder by clicking the Folder button beside this option.)
Forward	Forwards the message to another user. (Specify the user by clicking the To button.)
Reply With	Replies to the message with a standard response. (Specify the standard response by clicking the Template button to open a new Message form, and then use that **form** to write your standard response).
Custom	Responds to the message with a customized response. (Ask the **administrator** about these.)

Working with the Out Of Office Assistant

After you define the rules and describe the actions that the Out Of Office Assistant should take when it sees a message that, according to your rules, is one you're interested in, you click OK and the Out Of Office Assistant begins its work. Whenever you activate the Out Of Office Assistant and it then sees an interesting message, it performs whatever action you specified. You can use the Move Up and Move Down buttons in the Out Of Office Assistant dialog box to prioritize the rules and actions you specify.

Rules Wizard

PAB ⁘ Personal Address Book

Paragraph Alignment ⁘ Alignment

Password If your computer is connected to a network running Exchange Server, you must be logged onto the network to start the Outlook program. You can set it up so that when you log on to your network, you automatically log on to Outlook. To do so, choose Services from the Tools menu. In the Services dialog box, select Microsoft Exchange Server from the list of information services and click Properties. In the Microsoft Exchange Server dialog box, click the Advanced tab.

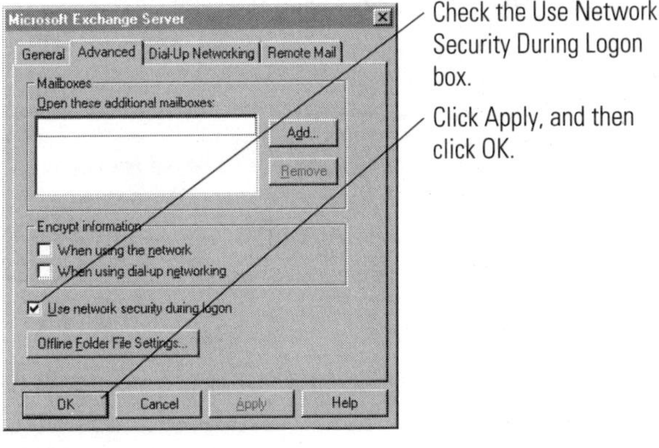

⁘ **Security**

Permission Within the Outlook environment, the term *permission* refers to someone's ability to noodle around with items in a **public folder**. To read **messages** in a public folder or **post messages** to a public folder, you must have permission. (The **administrator** gives permission.)

Personal Address Book With Outlook's **Address Book,** you can create your own personal list of people's **e-mail names** (and a whole bunch of other information as well). When you add someone's name and e-mail address to the Address Book, for example, that information actually goes into what's called a Personal Address Book.

To view the contents of your Personal Address Book, click the Address Book toolbar button so that Outlook displays the Address Book window. Then choose Personal Address Book from the Show Names From The list.

Personal Folder A personal folder is just a **folder** you use to store the **messages** you create and the messages you receive. Other users on your network can't read the messages in your personal folder.

Public Folder

Pop-Up Box A pop-up box looks like a message box, but it doesn't have a title bar, and it doesn't have a control menu. Help uses pop-up boxes to display its Help glossary definitions.

Post Message A post message, or post, is a special type of **message** that doesn't get delivered to a **recipient,** but rather gets delivered to a **folder**. In effect, post messages (which is what I call them) are very much like the announcements that people tack on the bulletin board at the local grocery store. You know the type I mean: the ones that advertise 11-year-old baby-sitters, '69 Camaros, and rewards for lost Labradors.

Post messages are a slick way to share information with other Outlook **users** without having to send everybody an individual message. By having a **public folder** that stores, for example, one copy of a company's holiday schedule, holiday information is always available to everybody and is easy to get.

Creating a Public Folder for Post Messages

To create a public folder for post messages (if one doesn't already exist), select the Public Folders folder and then choose New from the File menu. Then choose Folder from the submenu. When Outlook displays the Create New Folder dialog box, name the new folder, identify its contents, specify its location in the folder hierarchy, describe it briefly, and click OK. (You must have **permission** to do this.)

Writing a Post Message

To write a post message, select the folder to which you want to add the message. Then choose New Post In This Folder from the Compose menu. Outlook displays the Discussion form.

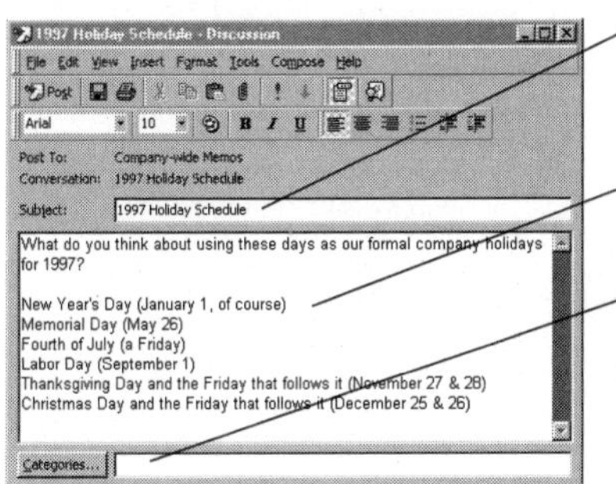

1 Describe your message in a word or two.

2 Type your message text here.

3 Assign your message to a **category**.

Attaching a File to a Post Message

It's easy to attach a **file** to a post message. You would do this, for example, when you want to share a file with people but don't want to waste disk space by e-mailing 300 people the same 1-megabyte file.

To attach a file to a post message, click the Insert File toolbar button. When Outlook displays the Insert File dialog box, use its boxes to name the file and identify its disk location.

Attaching Other Items to Your Post Message

You can attach any Outlook **item** to a post message. To do this, choose Item from the Insert menu. When Outlook displays the Insert Item dialog box, use it to identify the item you want to send.

continues

Post Message *(continued)*

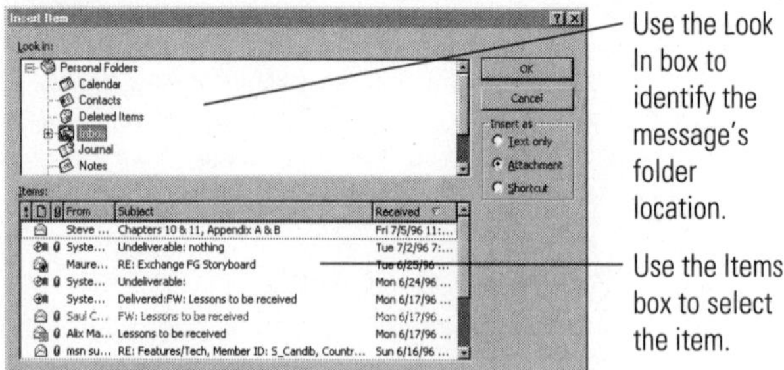

Specify how you want the item inserted.

Click OK to insert the item.

Posting a Message

After you write your post message, send it by clicking the Post button. Outlook places your post message in the folder you selected.

Reading Post Messages

To read the post messages in a folder, display the folder's contents list by clicking the folder's icon in the **Folder List**. Outlook lists any post messages in the folder. To view a post message, double-click it. When you do this, Outlook displays the post message.

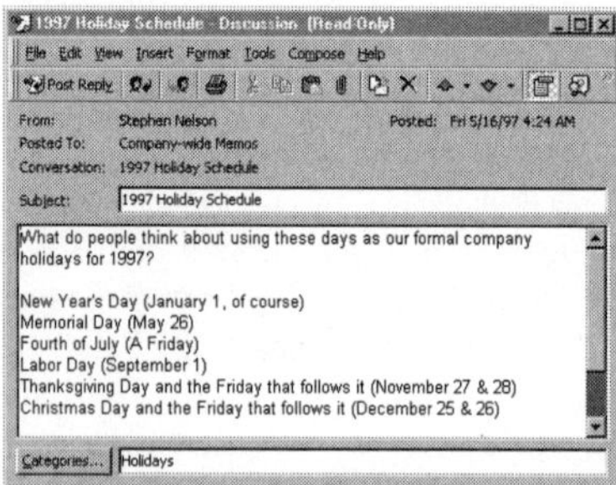

Group post messages by conversation thread

The easiest way to review post messages that were created in response to an original post message is to group the post messages by **conversation thread**. To do this, display the folder with the post messages you want to view and then choose Group By from the View menu. In the Group By dialog box, click Conversation in the Group Items By list.

Replying to Post Messages

You can reply to a post message in either of two ways: by replying directly to the post message sender or by posting another message.

To reply directly to the sender, click the Reply button. Outlook opens a new Message form that contains a copy of the original post message. Type in your reply, and click Send.

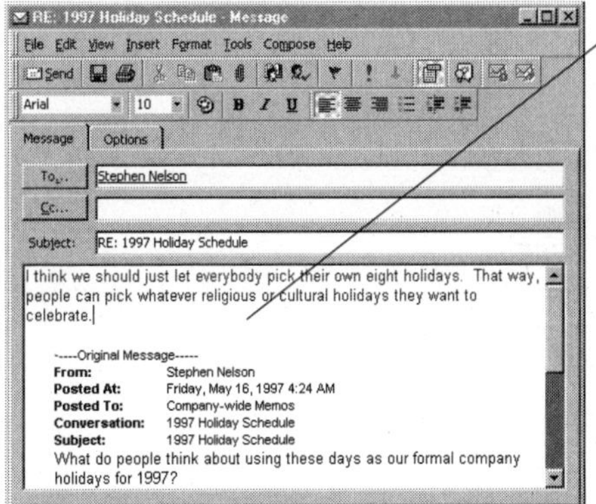

Type your reply here.

Click Send

To post another message, display the post message and then choose New Post In This Folder or Post Reply In This Folder from the Compose menu, or click the Post Reply toolbar button. Outlook opens a new Untitled—Discussion form. Type in your comment or reply, and click the Post button.

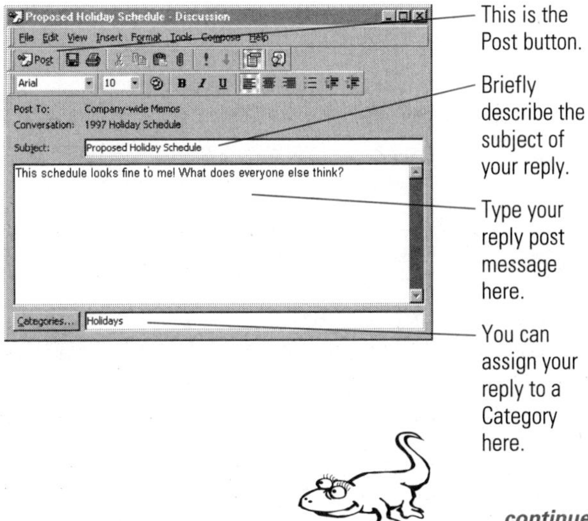

continues

Post Message *(continued)*

Forwarding a Message

If you read a post message that you want to forward to someone else, you can easily do so. First either click the post message in the **information viewer** or display the post message in a **form.** Next click the Forward button. After you click the Forward button, Outlook opens a new Message form that contains a copy of the original post message.

Specify to whom you want to forward the post message by entering an **e-mail name.**

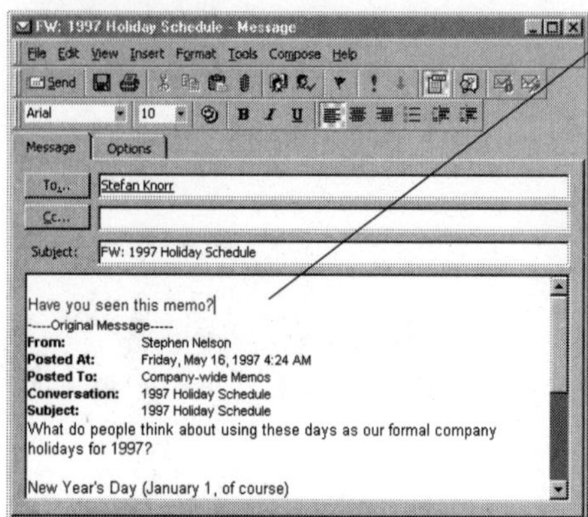

Add comments to the message by typing some more stuff in here.

Click the Send button when you want to send the message.

Printing a Post Message

You can print post messages in the same way you print regular messages. First display the post message. Then click the Print button.

If you want more control over how your message is printed, you can also choose Print from the File menu. When you choose this command, Outlook displays the Print dialog box. You can use it to choose a printer, specify the number of printed copies, describe what Outlook should do about any **attachments,** and so forth.

Priority See Importance

Private Appointments and Tasks You can mark an **appointment** or **task** private either when you create the appointment or task or later on, after you've created it. Making an appointment or task "private" so that others don't know about it may seem sort of funny, until you remember that other **users** may be able to view your schedule (as they need to do when they schedule meetings). What's more, you may not want your coworkers to know that you are visiting a doctor (because you're pregnant, say) or that you are involved in a confidential meeting (say, a discussion of employee bonuses).

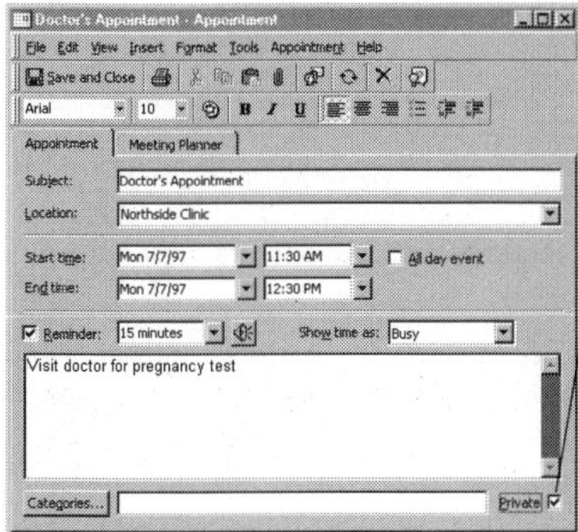

Check this box to make an appointment private.

After you've marked a task or appointment private, your coworkers can't see its details, even if they have **permission** to view your **Calendar** and **Task List.**

Viewing other Outlook users' calendars

If you want to know what your coworkers' schedules look like, you must get **delegate access** to view their Calendars. Once you've done so, choose Open Special Folder from the File menu, and then choose Exchange Server Folder. Click Name and select a name from the list in the Select Names dialog box. Click OK. Then select a Calendar from the Folder drop-down list box and click OK again. Outlook displays the Calendar of the person whose name you indicated.

continues

Private Appointments and Tasks *(continued)*

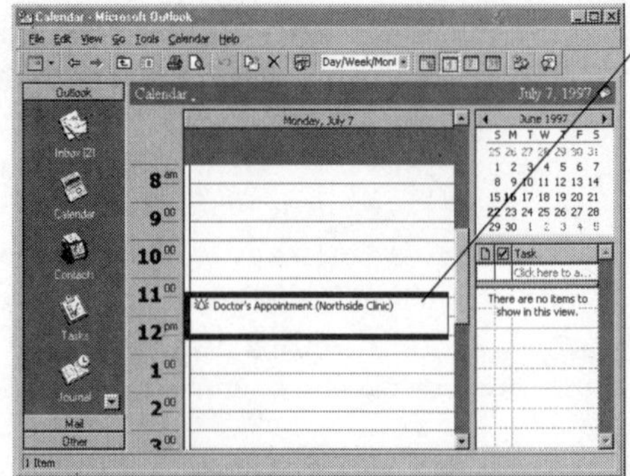

This is what an appointment looks like to you and other **network** users *before* you check the Private box.

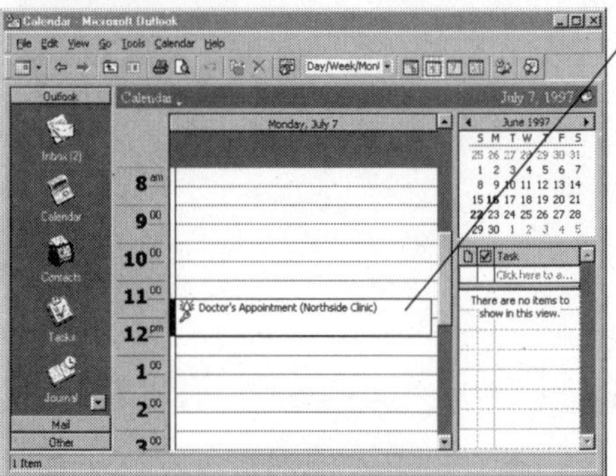

This is what an appointment looks like to you *after* you check the Private box.

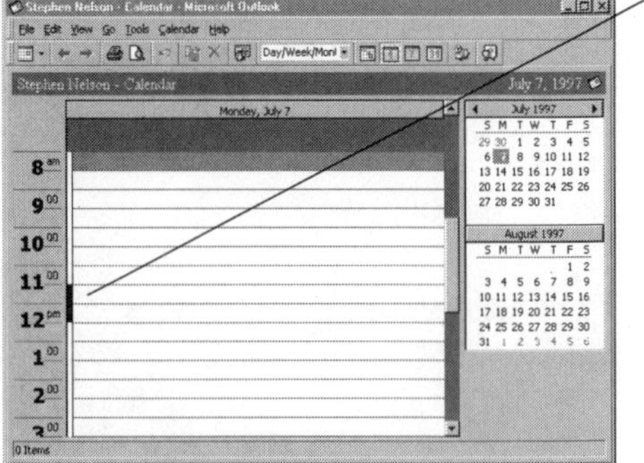

This is what an appointment looks like to other network users *after* you check the Private box.

Private text in your own schedule isn't hidden from you

The private text in your own Calendar and Task List isn't hidden from you. If you select an appointment or task, Outlook displays the appointment or task description.

Private Folder Outlook stores copies of the e-mail **messages** you send and receive in private folders because other people can't view the contents of private folders.

Public Folder

Program I use the term *program* to refer to software applications such as Outlook. I should confess that this is slightly kooky because technical types call these things "applications." My thought, however, is that any piece of software that you start by making a choice from the Programs menu in Windows 95 or using the Program Manager in Windows 3.x is, in fact, a program.

Program Window I use the term *program window* to refer to the window that appears when you start **programs.** I'm not sure whether calling them *program windows* is entirely kosher, however. Traditionally, these windows have been called *application windows*. But I think program window is a better term because Windows (and most nontechnical people) refer to software products like Outlook as *programs*. So it's really cleaner to call the windows these programs display program windows. At least that's what I think.

Public Folder Public folders are just places where you store **post messages** that you want a bunch of different people to see (or at least have access to). Typically, you store post messages in a public folder so you don't have to waste time sending a bunch of different people the same e-mail **message.**

Read and Unread Messages Both read and unread **messages** can be found in the **Inbox** or any other message folder (if you move them there or set up rules so that they go there instead of into the Inbox). To help you know which is which, Outlook displays unread message information in boldface characters and read message information in regular characters. Take a look at the following figure to see what I mean.

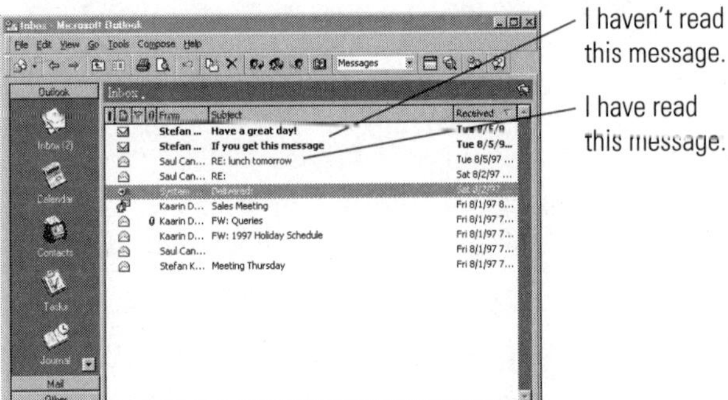

By the way, the Edit menu provides several commands for marking and unmarking read and unread messages. To use one of these commands, you simply click the message you want to mark or unmark. Then you choose the command.

Quick Reference: Edit Menu Commands

Read Receipt Do you work with people who mysteriously lose or never receive the e-mail **messages** you send them? You know what I mean. You're in some really important meeting with the Big Cheese, and you say something like, "Well, I did send Geoffrey an e-mail message about all this..." And Geoffrey, who always was kind of a slimeball, informs the Big Cheese, "I *never* got that message."

Read receipts are made for such occasions. While a **delivery receipt** confirms that a message got to a user's **mailbox,** a read receipt confirms that a **user** has actually opened the message. To ask the Exchange server to confirm that a message has been opened by the **recipient,** click the Options tab of the Message form while you're writing a message and then check Tell Me When This Message Has Been Read under Tracking Options.

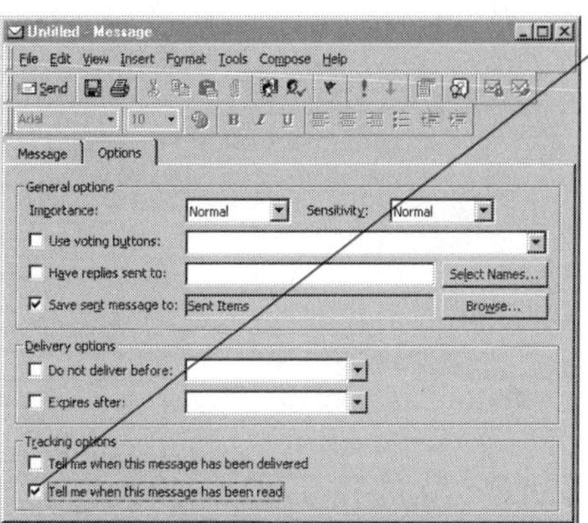

Check the Tell Me When This Message Has Been Read box to ask the Exchange server to tell you when the user reads the message.

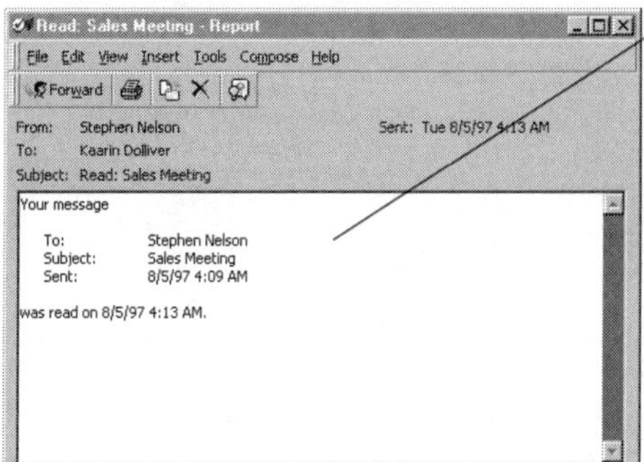

This is the message you receive, confirming that your message was opened.

continues

A word of warning

Read receipts and delivery receipts appear to be the perfect tools in **organizations** where paranoia and backbiting run rampant. Unfortunately, however, they triple the workload of your server because every message you create triggers the creation of two more messages from the server (the delivery receipt message and the read receipt message). And these extra messages slow down the system for everybody. I'm not going to tell you how to run your department. But I will say that there are probably better ways to deal with the Geoffreys of the world.

Recipient ⁘ Sender

Recurring Appointment

You can create what's called a recurring appointment. In effect, this is an **appointment** that you want Outlook to schedule at a recurring interval: every day at 1:00 PM, every Friday afternoon, and so on. To create a recurring appointment, choose New Recurring Appointment from the Calendar menu. When Outlook displays the Appointment Recurrence dialog box, use its buttons and boxes to describe the appointment and how often it recurs.

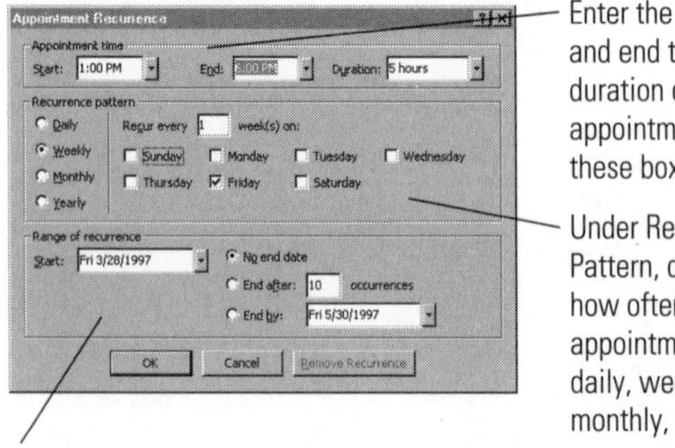

Enter the start time and end time or duration of the appointment in these boxes.

Under Recurrence Pattern, describe how often the appointment recurs: daily, weekly, monthly, and so forth.

You can use these buttons and boxes to specify the range of time over which the appointment recurs.

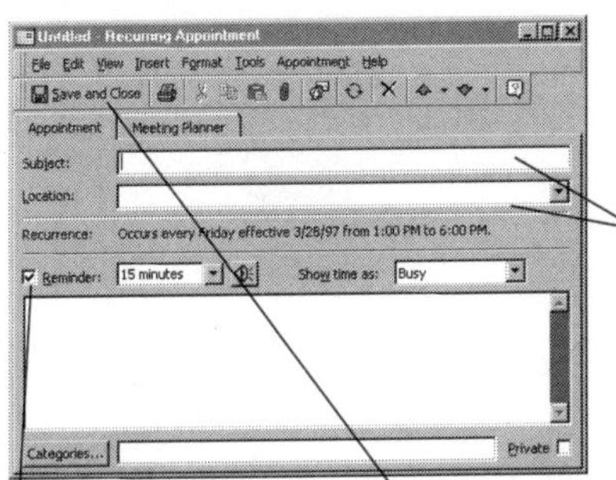

Click OK, and Outlook displays the Untitled-Recurring Appointment dialog box.

Describe the subject and location of the meeting using these boxes.

Set a reminder or make the appointment private using these boxes.

Click Save And Close to record the appointment in your calendar.

Making an existing appointment recurring

If you want to make an existing appointment a recurring appointment, double-click the appointment to display its Appointment dialog box. When you choose Recurrence from the Appointment menu, Outlook displays the Appointment Recurrence dialog box. You can use it to describe how often the appointment recurs.

Recurring Task

Recurring Task You can tell Outlook to place a recurring task on your **Task list.** For example, if you prepare a report every Friday afternoon, you can add the "Do report" task to every Friday's Task list.

To create a recurring task, choose Task from the New Task drop-down list. When Outlook displays the Task dialog box, use its boxes, buttons, and tabs to describe the task.

continues

Recurring Task *(continued)*

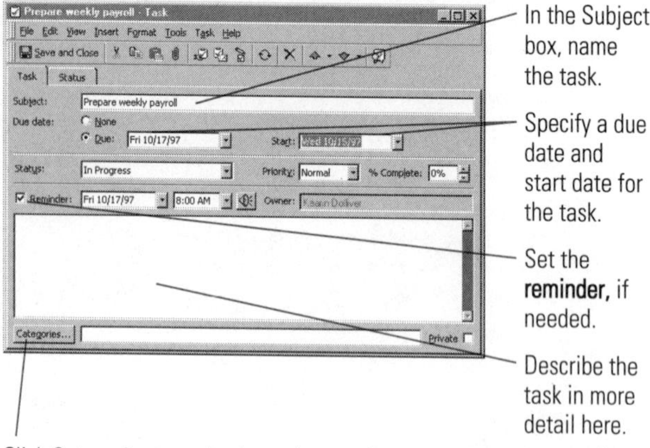

In the Subject box, name the task.

Specify a due date and start date for the task.

Set the **reminder,** if needed.

Describe the task in more detail here.

Click Categories to make the task part of a new or existing project. Then, to make the task recurring, choose Recurrence from the Task menu. Outlook displays the Task Recurrence dialog box.

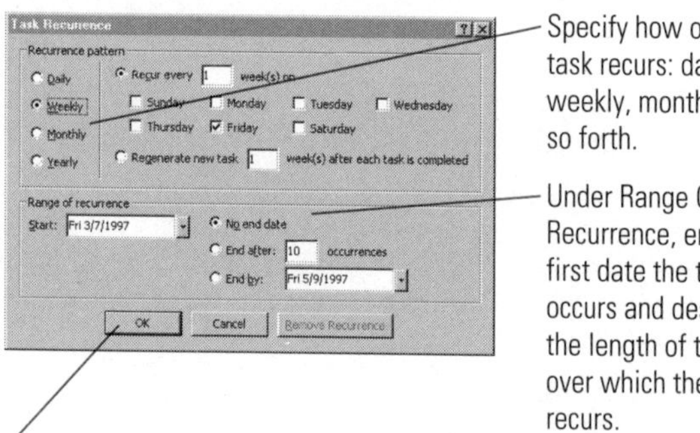

Specify how often the task recurs: daily, weekly, monthly, and so forth.

Under Range Of Recurrence, enter the first date the task occurs and describe the length of time over which the task recurs.

Click OK to record the task in your Task list.

Making an existing task recurring

If you want to make an existing task recurring, double-click it to display its Task dialog box. When you choose Recurrence from the Task menu, Outlook displays the Task Recurrence dialog box. You can use it to describe how often the task recurs.

Recurring Appointment

Reminder My grandmother, who is in her late eighties, has a system for remembering things. She writes herself a note and puts it in a coffee can on her nightstand. As long as she regularly reviews the contents of the coffee can, she gets to her appointments on time. Outlook has a reminder system too—and it probably works better than my grandma's. (Grandma, after all, needs to remember to sift through the contents of her coffee can.) If you want to be reminded about an upcoming **task** or **appointment,** you can double-click the task or appointment and then check the Reminder box in the dialog box. Outlook identifies the appointments and tasks it will remind you about with a little bell icon.

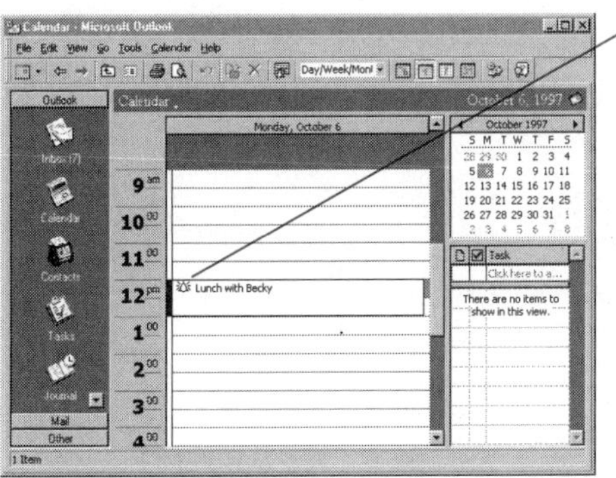

Ask not for whom the bell tolls. It tolls for thee.

Remote Mail Remote Mail lets you retrieve **messages** from your work computer to your home computer or to a laptop when you're on the road. Of course, to use remote mail, you must have Outlook installed on both your remote and office computers. In addition, they must be equipped with modems. And you need access to a telephone line, software to let you make a remote connection, and a mail delivery service like CompuServe, America Online, MSN, or an **Internet** service provider.

continues

Remote Mail *(continued)*

To use remote mail, choose Remote Mail from the Tools menu and then choose a command from the Remote Mail submenu. I'm not going to go into any great detail here about using remote mail. Suffice it to say that with remote mail, you can retrieve the messages in your **Inbox** from anywhere in the world. And you can save on connect time by first downloading only the message headers, so you can decide just which messages you want to read. Then you reconnect and retrieve in their entirety only the messages you want. The messages you deem unimportant can wait until you return to your office.

Using offline folders

If your network uses Microsoft Exchange Server, you have the option of using **offline folders** instead of, or in addition to, remote mail to make a remote connection. Offline folders give you several advantages over remote mail, including the ability to work with all of your Outlook folders, not just the Inbox.

Synchronize

Reply

You can respond to a **message** you receive with a new, or reply, message. To do this, select or display the message to which you want to respond and then click either the Reply or the Reply To All button. Outlook opens the **Message form,** which you use to create your response.

Rules and Actions

The **Inbox Assistant** and the **Out Of Office Assistant** use rules and actions to monitor and process incoming **messages.** For example, you might create a rule that tells Outlook to look for messages from your boss, and then you might specify an action for Outlook to take when it finds a message, such as to play a special sound.

Rules Wizard

Rules Wizard The Rules Wizard helps you set rules that determine actions that Outlook will take automatically when certain conditions are met. For example, you can use the Rules Wizard to define an "important message," and then tell Outlook to notify you when an important message arrives by displaying a special pop-up announcement.

The Rules Wizard is intended to be a "plug-in" addition to Outlook. If you don't already have the Rules Wizard on your computer, you can download it (and maybe some other goodies, too,) from the Microsoft Web site at *http://www.microsoft.com.*

Using the Rules Wizard to Create a New Rule

To use the Rules Wizard to create a new rule, choose Rules Wizard from the Tools menu. Outlook displays the first Rules Wizard dialog box. Click New. Then follow these steps:

1 In the first Rules Wizard dialog box, choose the type of rule you want to create. Indicate when you want to apply the rule, and then click Next.

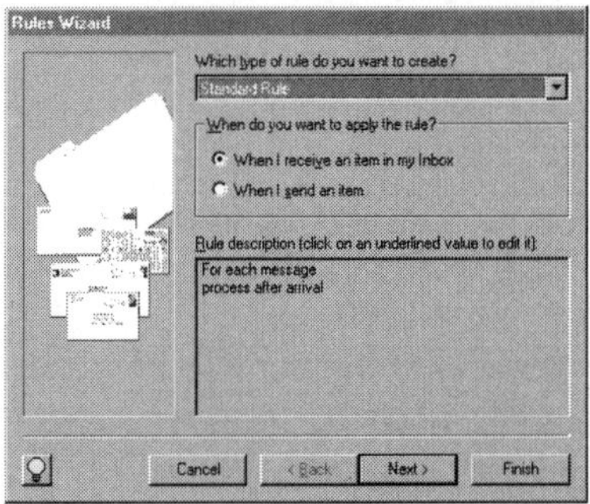

2 In the second Rules Wizard dialog box, check the condition(s) you want Outlook to watch for. Then click Next.

continues

Rules Wizard *(continued)*

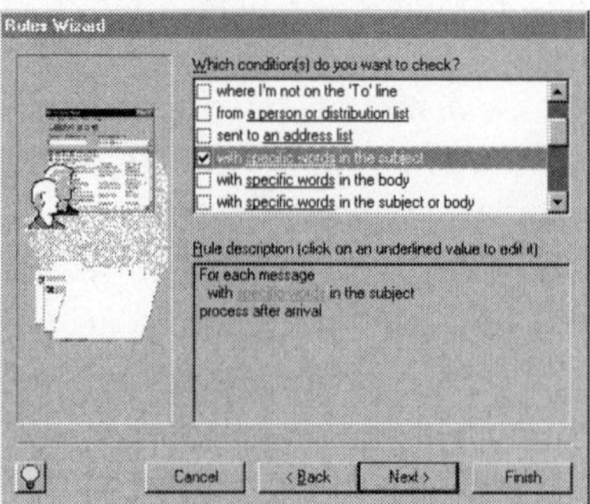

3 In the third Rules Wizard dialog box, indicate the actions you want Outlook to take when the condition(s) you set are met.

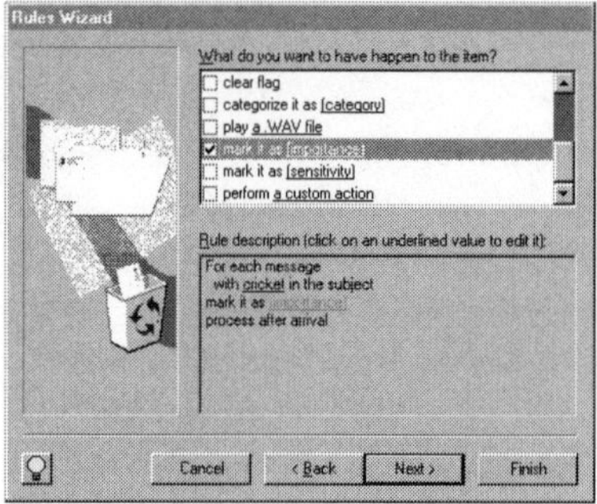

4 In the fourth Rules Wizard dialog box, indicate any exceptions to the rule.

5 In the final Rules Wizard dialog box, name the rule, check the Turn On This Rule box, and click Finish.

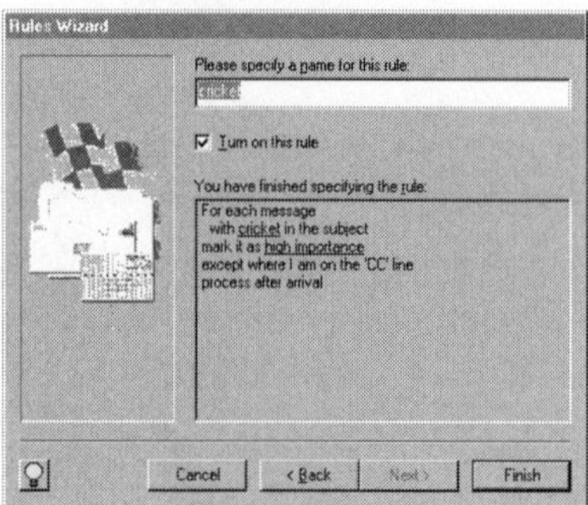

Customizing Rules

In any of the Rules Wizard dialog boxes, just click on any underlined text in the Rule Description box to customize that text. For example, click on the underlined words in "sent to an address list" and change them to "John Doe." (When you select an item containing underlined text in the upper text box, the text becomes available for editing in the Rule Description box.)

Using the Rules Wizard to Apply an Existing Rule

After you've created a rule by using the Rules Wizard or Out Of Office Assistant, you can apply (or disable) any rule by choosing Rules Wizard from the Tools menu. Outlook will display the first Rules Wizard dialog box, which lists all existing rules and lets you apply or disable them by checking or unchecking boxes. You can also change the order in which rules are applied by using the Move buttons.

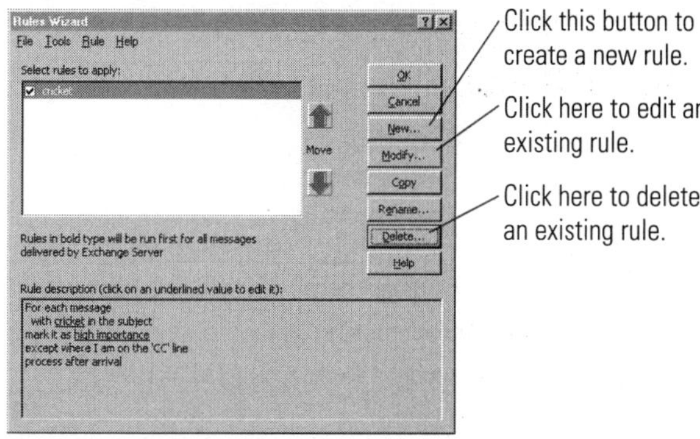

Inbox Assistant; Out Of Office Assistant; Rules and Actions

Schedule+ Schedule+ is another of the time-management components of the Exchange family of products. Using Schedule+, people can schedule appointments and meetings, keep a To Do list, and organize projects. Since Outlook, in many ways, replaces Schedule+, and since this book is about Outlook, I won't say much about Schedule+. However, you should know that if you're hooked on Schedule+, you can still use it as your main scheduling program. To do so, choose Options from the Tools menu. Check the Use Microsoft Schedule+ 7.0 As My Primary Calendar box.

Sealed Message As long as the Exchange server is configured the right way and Advanced Security is set up on the sender's and recipients' Outlook clients, you can seal a **message** by using a **digital signature.** A digital signature allows message **recipients** to be certain who sent a message and be absolutely sure that no one tampered with it en route.

Encryption; Security

Second Time Zone As an author, I often work with editors and publishers in other time zones. It is difficult to schedule **appointment** times with these people. You might think I could just add or subtract hours from my time, but that doesn't work. Some locations observe daylight saving time; others don't. And then, at least for me, things get really tricky when I'm working with someone on the other side of the international date line.

How a Second Time Zone Helps

Thankfully, Outlook provides a feature for straightening out these time considerations: you can add a second time zone's information to your daily **Calendar**. In this way, it's easy to describe an appointment by using times either in your time zone or that of the person you are dealing with.

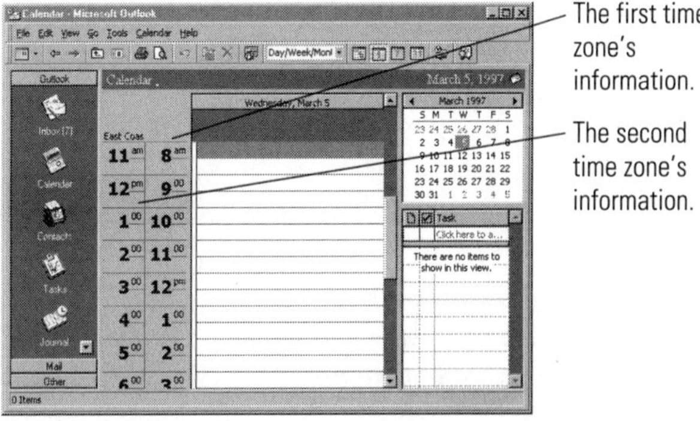

Adding a Second Time Zone

To add a second time zone, choose Options from the Tools menu and click the Time Zone button on the Calendar tab. Check the Show Another Time Zone When Viewing Days box to add a second set of appointment times to your daily Calendar.

To describe the second time zone, use the buttons and boxes of the Time Zone dialog box.

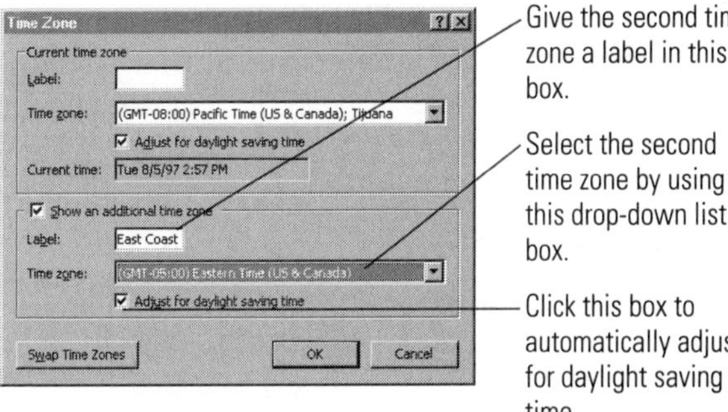

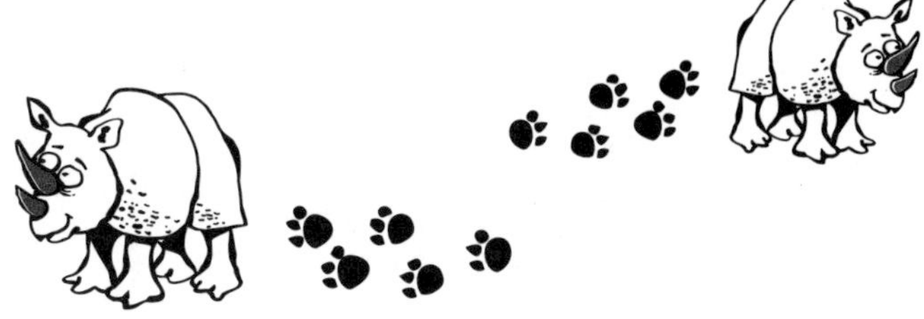

Security Outlook provides a bunch of different tools to make **e-mail** communications more secure. You can, for example, add **digital signatures** to **messages** so that **recipients** and readers can be sure who messages came from and be sure as well that messages weren't tampered with. You can also encrypt messages so that they can't be read by recipients who don't know the **encryption** code.

To use any of these security tools, the security features must be installed on the **server** and enabled for the sender's **client** and all the recipients' clients.

Sender The sender is the person who creates and distributes a **message.** If I jot off a quick message to you suggesting lunch next Friday, for example, I'm the sender. You are the recipient.

Sensitivity You can assign different levels of sensitivity to **messages.** By doing so, **recipients** can tell how important a message is and how it should be treated. To assign a sensitivity level to a message, click the Options tab in the **Message form.** Then use the Sensitivity drop-down list box to select a sensitivity level: Normal, Personal, Private, or Confidential.

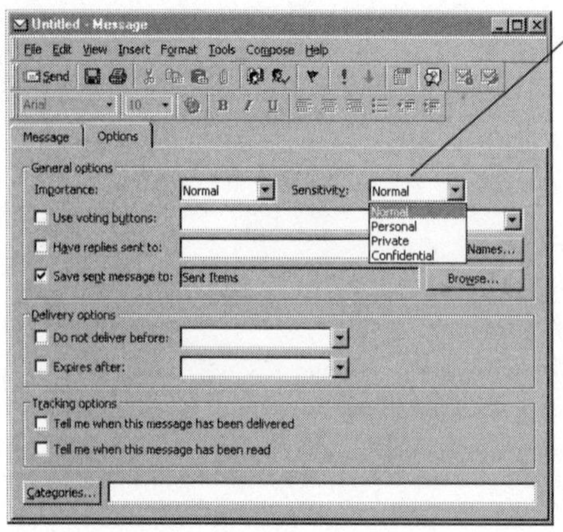

Message sensitivity information appears in the Sensitivity column of the **information viewer,** if that column is displayed.

How sensitivity affects messages

For the most part, message sensitivity doesn't affect anything. All it does is help recipients tell what kind of messages they've been sent. However, the Private sensitivity level is slightly different from the other three in that private messages, when they are forwarded or replied to, can't be edited. In other words, if you mark a message as private, the recipient can still **reply** to or **forward** it. But Outlook doesn't let the recipient change the private message in any way when he or she forwards or replies to it.

Server

In most **networks,** there are two kinds of computers: **clients** and servers. A client is what sits on top of or alongside people's desks. A server is what sits in the computer room or over in the corner of the office. The relationship between a client and a server is very much like the relationship between a diner and a waitress. The diner continually bugs the waitress with requests: "Cheese omelet," "More coffee," "Check please." On a computer network, the requests made by the client to the server are a little bit different: "Save this file," "Print this report," "Distribute these e-mail messages." But the process is very similar in both situations. The server's job is to quickly and efficiently respond to all of the questions and requests from each of the clients being served.

I should mention one other thing about clients and servers while we're on the subject. If your computer is part of a network, much of the software you use has both a client and a server component. Take, for example, the case of Outlook. The windows, **forms,** and dialog boxes that you see on your computer screen are displayed and controlled by the **Outlook client,** which is the software **program** running on your computer. The program that does the dirty work of passing **messages** around the network is actually Microsoft Exchange Server, which is the software program running on the server computer.

Smiley As a means of communication, **e-mail** has certain drawbacks. Even with really good writers (so I hear), it's easy for comments to be misinterpreted and for nuances to be lost. For these reasons, a lot of people use what are called smileys in their **messages.** A smiley is a combination of punctuation characters that, taken together, form a smiley face, a frowning face, or another kind of face.

You'll see smileys in your correspondence, so I'm not going to provide examples of them here (they don't look all that great in books like this anyway). Before I close this little digression, however, I want to mention what happens to smileys when you enter them with **Microsoft Word.** If Word is your e-mail editor—and there's a good chance it is—Word takes the smiley faces and frowning faces that you build with punctuation marks and replaces them with equivalent characters from the Wingdings dingbat font. (A dingbat font is just a font with a bunch of crazy characters.)

One of Smiley's people.

Not one of Smiley's people.

SMTP SMTP is the acronym for simple mail transport protocol. SMTP is the set of rules and conventions that Outlook uses to pass e-mail **messages** to the **Internet**. You see this acronym used a few places in Outlook, but you don't really need to know anything about it.

Sorting You can sort items in any Outlook **folder**. For example, Outlook lists **messages** in your **information viewer** in the order in which they were sent. But you can sort messages in other ways, for instance, by sender name or by message subject. To do this, choose Sort from the View menu. When Outlook displays the Sort dialog box, use the Sort Items By and Then By boxes and the Ascending and Descending buttons to specify how you want messages sorted.

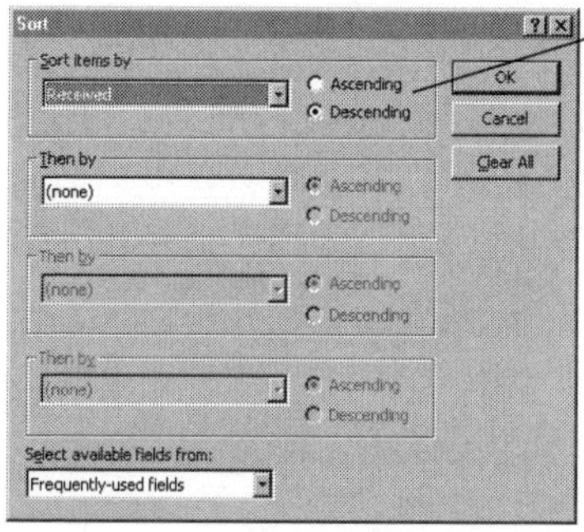

Specify how you want messages arranged by using the Sort Items By drop-down list box.

Speed Dial Speed Dial lets you create a list of phone numbers that you frequently call and then dial those numbers using your computer. Of course, you have to have a modem to take advantage of Speed Dial. But if you do, it's pretty neat—similar to the feature that you find on some telephones but with unlimited memory for numbers.

Adding Numbers to the Speed Dial Menu

To add numbers to the Speed Dial menu, choose Dial from the Tools menu. Then choose New Call. Outlook displays the New Call dialog box. Click Dialing Options, and Outlook displays the Dialing Options dialog box.

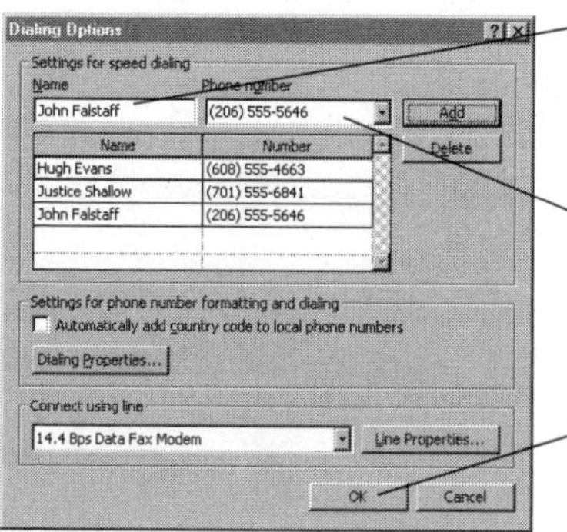

In the Name box, type the name of the person you want to add to the Speed Dial list.

In the Phone Number box, type the phone number of the person you want to add to the Speed Dial list.

Click Add and OK.

continues

Speed Dial *(continued)*

Using Speed Dial to Place a Call

To dial a number on the Speed Dial list, choose Dial on the Tools menu and then Speed Dial on the Dial submenu. Select the number you want to call from the Speed Dial menu. In the Dial Phone dialog box, click Start Call, pick up the receiver, and then click Talk in the Call Status dialog box. When you complete your call, click Hang Up, replace the receiver, and click End Call in the Dial Phone dialog box. Then pick another number from the Dial Number drop-down list, or if you have no other calls to make, click Close.

Spelling Checker

You can—and you should—use Outlook's spelling checker to correct spelling errors in your e-mail messages. Misspelled words in messages make a bad impression. To check the spelling of the words in a message, choose Spelling from the Tools menu. If Outlook finds a misspelled word, it displays the Spelling dialog box.

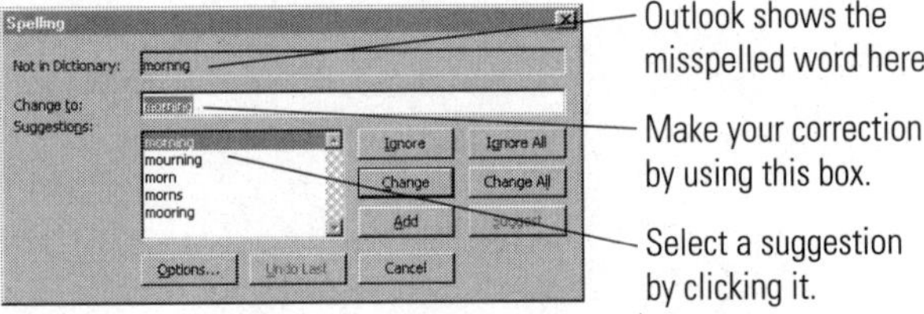

Spelling Buttons

The buttons in the Spelling dialog box assist in spell-checking and error-correction.

Button	What it does
Ignore	Ignores only this occurrence of the word.
Ignore All	Ignores this and every other occurrence of the word.
Change	Changes this occurrence of the word to what the Change To box shows.
Change All	Changes this and every other occurrence of the word to what the Change To box shows.
Add	Adds the word to the spelling dictionary.
Suggest	Looks for similarly spelled words in the spelling dictionary.

Spelling Options

You can control, to a minor extent, the way in which Outlook's spelling checker works. To do this, choose Options from the Tools menu and click the Spelling Tab. Or with the Spelling dialog box on your screen, click the Options button.

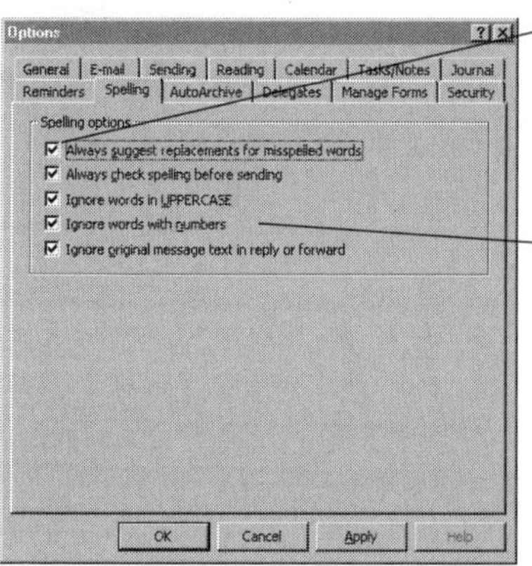

The first two options are pretty self-explanatory. I recommend checking both of these boxes.

The Ignore options (the last three) let you weed out word and character strings that aren't going to appear in any dictionary—such as proper nouns, kooky acronyms, and alphanumeric codes. You can also tell Outlook to ignore the original text.

Check Names

Status Bar The status bar appears along the bottom edge of the Outlook **program window.** In the Outlook program window, the status bar tells you how many **items** are in the **folder** you selected. (If you don't see the status bar, click Status Bar on the View menu.)

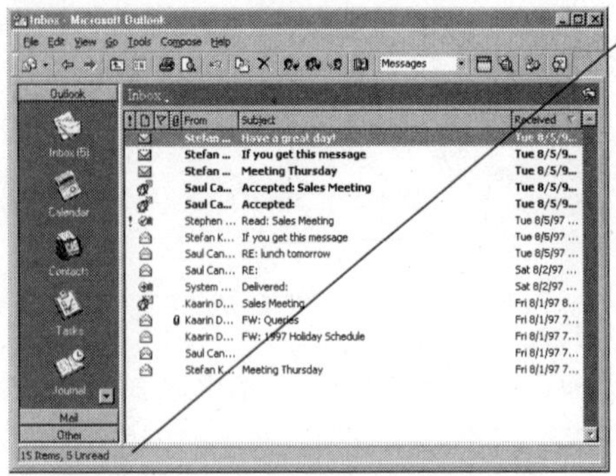

The Outlook client status bar summarizes the messages in the selected folder.

Subfolder A subfolder is a **folder** within a folder. Using subfolders is a good way to organize your **messages** better.

Subject When you create a **message,** you have the option of including a brief description of the message's subject. I recommend including meaningful subject descriptions with messages. They make it easier for people to **sort** and **filter** messages. By including a subject, you increase the chances of someone saving your message for future reference. And **recipients** will probably read your messages sooner.

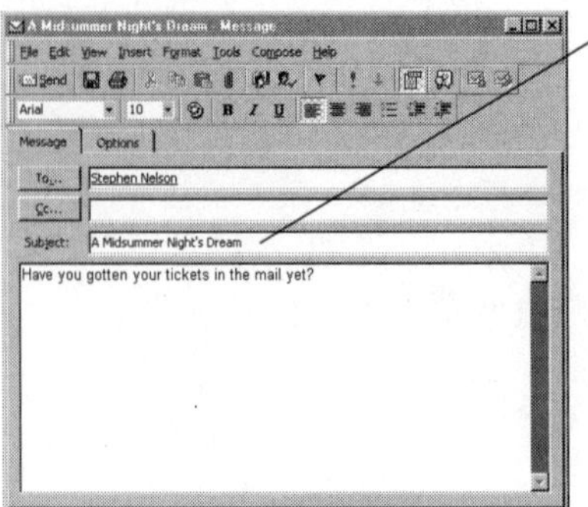

Here's where you enter the message subject. As soon as you do, Outlook renames the **Message form** using the subject.

Synchronize If you work with **offline folders,** you will need to synchronize your online and offline folders when you log on to your network. When you synchronize your folders, any changes you make while using your folders offline are incorporated into your online folders so that both sets of folders are identical. To synchronize folders, choose Synchronize from the Tools menu and then choose All Folders from the submenu.

Remote Mail

Task Filters Outlook lets you filter the tasks in the **Task List** so you can decide which tasks appear in the list. For example, you can show only tasks that you haven't yet finished. Or tasks that you should have finished by now but haven't. Or even tasks that you haven't yet started. You perform this filtering by choosing Filter from the View menu.

Folder View

Task List **Tasks**

TaskPad The TaskPad is the mini-tasks list you see in the lower right corner of the **Calendar** folder. When you add a new task to the TaskPad, it shows up on the main Task List in the **Tasks** folder.

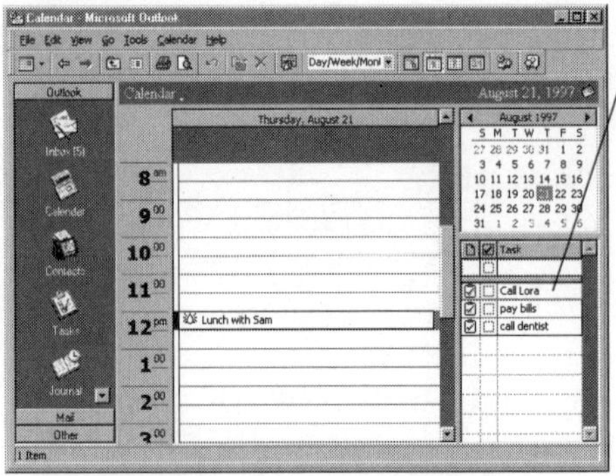

This is the TaskPad.

Use the TaskPad View submenu commands on the View menu to choose which tasks appear. You can drag a task from the TaskPad onto the Calendar to schedule work on the task.

Tasks Outlook lets you build a list of the things—called tasks—you're supposed to get done. You can organize tasks into projects by grouping them into **categories,** or you can **group** them by a variety of other criteria. You can **filter** tasks to select certain ones, **sort** tasks in the Task list, and drag tasks to move them up and down in the Task list. You can assign tasks to your coworkers, track the progress you've made on completing tasks, and send reports to your colleagues describing the **task status.**

Adding a Task to Your Task List

To add a task to your Task list, start Outlook and click the Tasks icon in the **Outlook Bar**. Then click the top line of the Task list in the Subject **field** (where it says *Click here to add new task*).

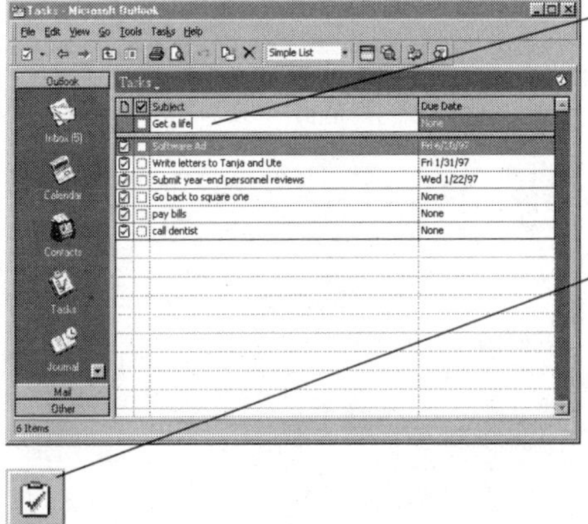

Type a short description of the task into an empty row.

Alternatively, to provide more detailed information about a task you're adding, click the New Task toolbar button.

Outlook displays the Task dialog box. Then use the tabs, buttons, and boxes in the Task dialog box to describe the task in detail.

Viewing Your Task List

Outlook supplies ten predefined **views** of the Task list, including Simple List, Detailed List, Active Tasks, Completed Tasks, and Task Timeline. Choose a view using the toolbar View Selector drop-down list, or use the Define Views command on the View menu to create a custom view.

Assigning a Task

If you have the authority, you can assign tasks to your coworkers using Outlook. Double-click an existing task on the Task List, or click the New Task toolbar button to open a new Task form.

continues

Tasks *(continued)*

In the Task form, choose Assign Task from the Task menu. Outlook displays an altered Task form.

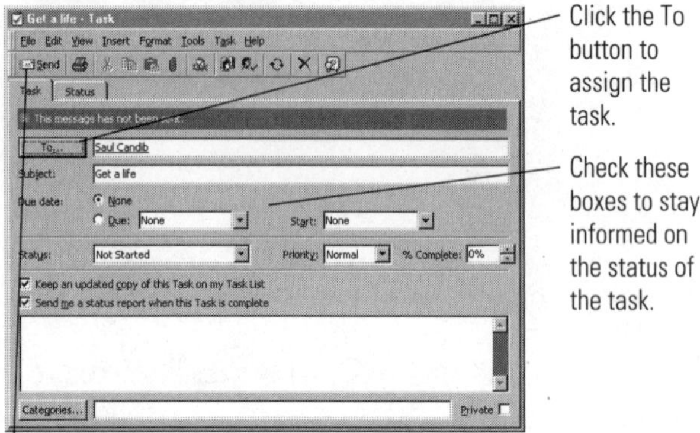

The person to whom you assign the task can accept, decline, or re-assign the task request.

Accepting, Declining, and Reassigning Tasks

If you are assigned a task, you can accept it by clicking Accept. Outlook displays the Accepting Task dialog box. You can simply accept a task, or you can accept it and add a comment. To accept a task without adding a comment, click Send The Response Now in the Accepting Task dialog box and then click OK. To add a comment, click Edit The Response Before Sending in the Accepting Task dialog box and then click OK. Write your response, and then click Send. When you accept a task, you become the "owner" of the task.

To decline a task you have been assigned, click Decline. Outlook displays the Declining A Task dialog box. To decline a task without adding a comment, click Send The Response Now in the Declining Task dialog box and then click OK. To add a comment, click Edit The Response Before Sending in the Declining Task dialog box and then click OK. Write your response, and then click Send. (You can say, "Thanks, but no thanks," or "I quit!") The task is returned to the person who sent it to you.

To reassign a task, open the message that contains the task request. Click Assign Task, and use the To box to name the person to whom you want to assign the task. Then click Send. The new task recipient then has the option of accepting, declining, or reassigning the task.

Categorizing and Prioritizing Tasks

To assign a task to a **category,** click the Category button and choose a category from the list in the Categories dialog box or create a new category. Then click OK.

To prioritize a task, display the Priority drop-down list and choose Normal, High, or Low priority from the list. High-priority tasks are marked with a red exclamation point in the Detailed List task view.

Recurring Task; Task Status

Task Status

You can track the status of a task you are working on and let other members of your workgroup know the task status. Tasks can be assigned the status Not Started, In Progress, Completed, Waiting On Someone Else, or Deferred. In addition, you can indicate the percent completion of a task and note the total and actual work done on a task.

Tracking the Status of a Task

Double-click to display a task in your Task List, or click the New Task button to open a new Task form. On the Task tab, choose a status from the Status drop-down list, and use the % Complete spin box to indicate the percentage of the task already completed. Then click the Status tab.

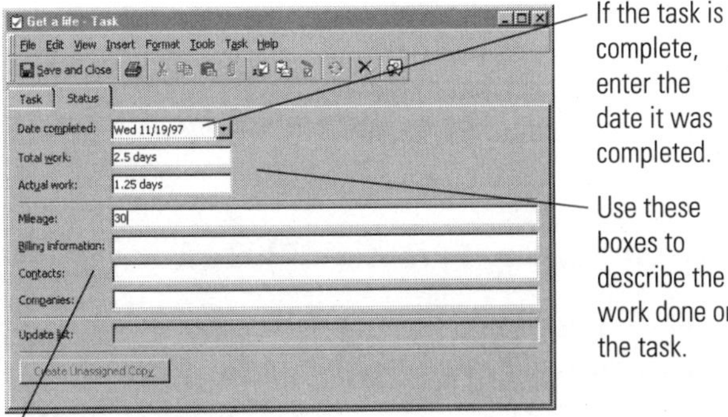

If the task is complete, enter the date it was completed.

Use these boxes to describe the work done on the task.

Use these boxes to enter additional information about the work done on the task.

continues

Task Status *(continued)*

Sending a Task Status Report

To send a task status report, double-click the task in the Task List to display the task form. Choose Send Status Report from the task menu. Outlook displays the Task Status Report—Message form.

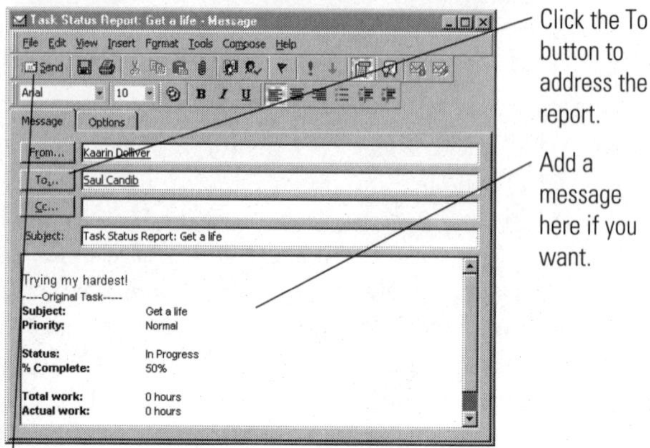

Click the To button to address the report.

Add a message here if you want.

Click Send to deliver the report.

Tentative Appointments Tentative appointments show up in your appointment **Calendar,** but they aren't considered **busy time.** As a result, an **appointment** that you mark as tentative doesn't preclude the **Meeting Planner** from scheduling a meeting for the same time as the tentative appointment.

Thread *see* **Conversation Thread**

Time Zone *see* **Second Time Zone**

To Do List Outlook lets you keep an online To Do list, which it calls a **Task List.** With the list, you can keep track of the **tasks** you're supposed to do but haven't yet done. That report for your boss. The telephone call to the sales guys in Atlanta. A birthday present for your daughter.

Reminder; TaskPad

Toolbar Outlook features toolbars to make things easier for you. (A toolbar is just a group of clickable buttons.) Because it's usually easier to click a button than choose a command, I emphasize the toolbar way in this little book. A picture of a toolbar button appears in the margin whenever I direct you to click one so that you don't have any trouble finding the button on your screen. Like all the other applications in Office 97, Outlook has menus that display toolbar button icons next to menu commands to help you remember the association. By the way, if your **program window** doesn't show a toolbar, choose the View Toolbar command.

Quick Reference: Toolbar Buttons

Undo You can undo your last editing change to a **message.** To do this, choose Undo from the Edit menu. I feel like I should say more about Undo. But there's no sense, really, in making something that is so easy more complicated. Remember Ockham's razor!

Unread Messages **Read and Unread Messages**

URL

The URL, short for Uniform Resource Locator, specifies how you find an **Internet** resource such as a **World Wide Web** page. A URL has four parts: the service, or protocol; the server name; the path; and the document, or file, name.

A Sample URL Explained

Let me explain what each of these things is, using a real-life **Web page**—the one that provides biographical data on the President of the United States and his family. Here it is:

http://www.whitehouse.gov/White_House/html/Life.html

http:// identifies this resource as part of the World Wide Web

www.whitehouse.gov/ identifies the server

White_House/html/ names the directory and subdirectory of the World Wide Web document

Life.html names the World Wide Web document

Hyperlink; HTML

Users

Users are just the people who use Outlook. (In particular, they're the ones who use it as a network **client**.) Regular folk like you and me.

Administrator

Uuencode

Some e-mail systems (although thankfully not Outlook) don't let you include files in your e-mail **message.** With these systems, you can only send text.

Okay. I know what you're thinking. Not being able to attach a nontext file to an e-mail message seems like a pretty big limitation. And you're right. So to deal with this limitation, people created a **program** called Uuencode (pronounced you-you-n-code). It converts, or encodes, nontext files to text files so that they can be included in e-mail messages such as those sent over the Internet. At the other end, when the **recipient** gets the message, the program converts, or decodes, the text files and turns them back into nontext files.

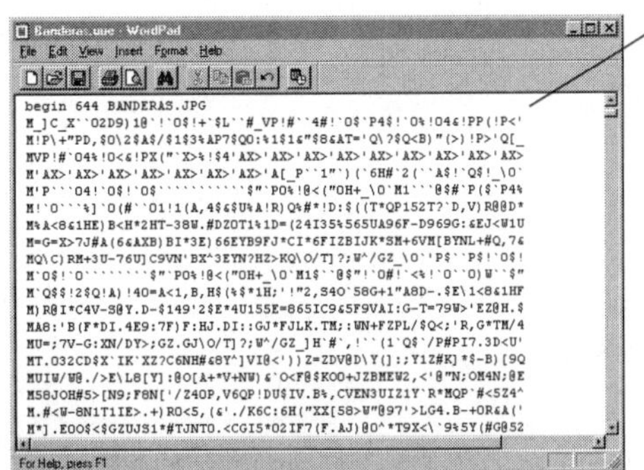

Believe it or not, this is actually a Uuencoded picture of Antonio Banderas. Nice, huh?

You now know more than you need to about Uuencode. Outlook takes care of encoding and decoding Internet e-mail **attachments** automatically. And Outlook uses something called **MIME** for e-mail attachments you send and receive within your local network and between other systems that are smart enough to also use MIME.

Views

Each Outlook **folder** comes with several different views. A view organizes the **items** in a folder by specifying which **fields** appear, how items should be grouped or sorted, and whether any **filters** should be used. Views can be divided into several view types. Some view types are best suited for particular Outlook items.

You can choose one of the standard views, or you can modify a standard view or define an entirely new view. You modify views and define new views by choosing Define Views from the Views menu. You can save the new views you create so you can use them again.

Reviewing Outlook View Types

Outlook defines five view types: Table, Timeline, Card, Day/Week/Month, and Icon. View types determine the structure for how information will be displayed in a view. The following table gives a description of each view type and the folder where it is applied.

continues

Views *(continued)*

View Type	Description and where it is normally used
Table	Displays each item in its own row, and lists item details in columns. Used in the Inbox and the Tasks List and to show details about items in other folders.
Timeline	Displays items as icons in chronological order on a time scale. Used for Journal Entries and to display tasks, appointments, and other items chronologically.
Day/Week/Month	Displays appointments, meetings, events, and tasks as blocks of time in the Calendar. Used only in the Calendar.
Card	Displays items alphabetically as Rolodex-type address cards. Used in the Contact list.
Icon	Displays items and files as icons in an otherwise blank window. Used for Notes and for files in My Computer, My Documents, and Favorites.

Reviewing the Standard Inbox Views

Outlook provides a slew of standard, or predefined, views, including those Inbox views described in the table that follows. Many of these views, by the way, offer pretty much the same message information (Importance, Item Type, Attachment, From, Subject, Received, Size, Flag Status), although the different views do arrange the columns of the **information viewer** in different ways.

View	How it organizes messages
Messages	**Sorts messages** in the order received (with the most recent message appearing first), but doesn't filter or **group** messages.
Messages With AutoPreview	Same as Messages, but displays the first few lines of each message.
By Message Flag	Sorts messages in the order of when a response is due (with the most urgent response date appearing first), and groups messages by flag status.
Last Seven Days	Same as Messages, except filters messages to display only those received within the last week.

View	How it organizes messages
Flagged For Next Seven Days	Sorts messages by when a reply or other response is due. Filters messages to display only those flagged as needing a reply or other response.
By Sender	Sorts messages in the order received (with the most recent message appearing first) and groups messages by **sender,** but doesn't filter messages.
Unread Messages	Same as Messages, except filters messages to display only those that you haven't read yet (or that you've marked as unread).
Sent To	Sorts messages in the order received (with the most recent message appearing first). Groups messages by whom they were sent to. (Most messages in your Inbox probably were sent to you!)
Message Timeline	Sorts messages in the order received and displays them along a horizontal timeline (similar to that in the **Journal**).

Modifying a Standard View

You can modify standard Outlook views to suit your preferences and needs. Display a standard view and choose Define Views from the View menu. When Outlook displays the Define Views dialog box, click Modify. Outlook displays the View Summary dialog box, which summarizes the current view settings.

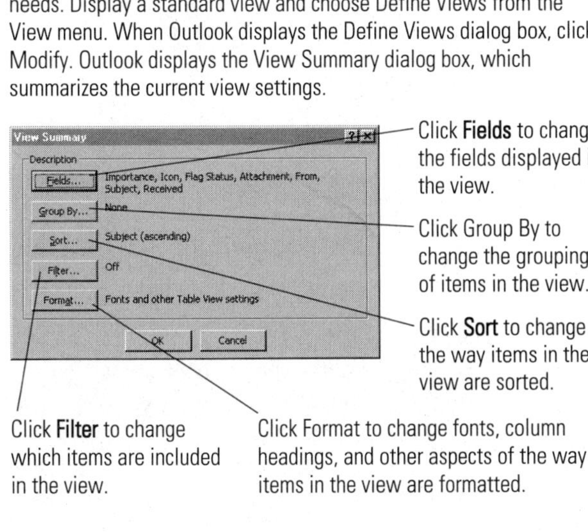

continues

Views *(continued)*

Defining a New View

The standard views that Outlook initially provides may be the only ones you need. But you can easily create your own views. Choose Define Views from the View menu. When Outlook displays the Define Views dialog box, click the New button. Outlook displays the Create A New View dialog box.

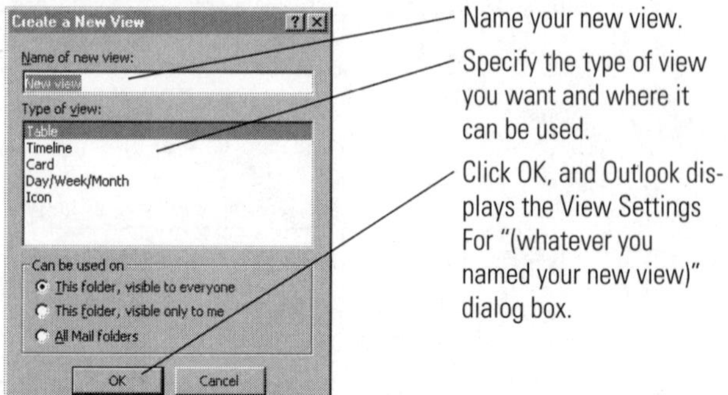

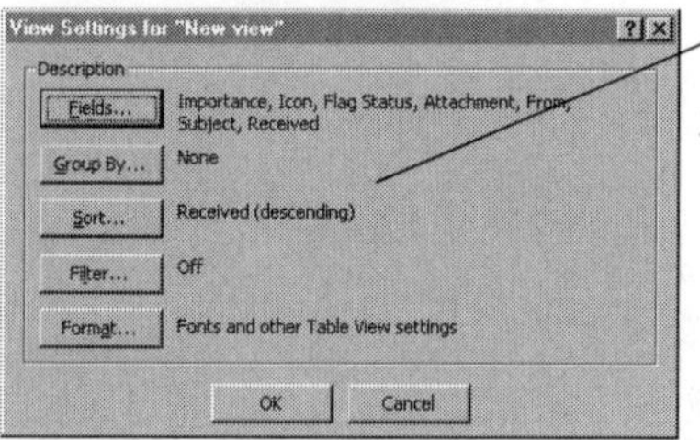

Click these buttons to specify the columns of message information, grouping, sorting, and filtering you want in your new view. Click OK when you're done.

Click Apply View and Close in the Define Views dialog box to see your new view.

Changing the View

To change the view, point to Current View on the View menu and then choose a view from the submenu.

Columns; Message Flag

Web Browser A Web browser is a program that lets you look at **World Wide Web** documents. Netscape and NCSA Mosaic are browsers, as is Microsoft Internet Explorer, which comes with Office 97. Most browsers let you browse, or view, both the graphics and text components of World Wide Web documents, but there are also browsers that let you look just at the text. (You might want to do this, for example, if your connection to the Internet is slow—say, less than 28.8 Kbps—or if you're really only interested in the text portions of the documents you are viewing.)

Web Page

Web Page Web page is another name for a document on the **World Wide Web,** the most popular part of the **Internet.** Web pages often combine text, graphics, and other elements, including sound and movie or video clips. Web pages also usually include **hyperlinks,** or jumps, to other Web pages. If you have access to the Internet and a Web browser, you can display the Web page of a selected contact in your **Contact list** by clicking the Explore Web Page toolbar button.

Word **Microsoft Word**

WordMail The Use Microsoft Word As E-Mail Editor check box on the Mail tab of the Options dialog box (choose Options from the Tools menu) lets you specify which text editor you want to use for writing Outlook messages. If you choose **Microsoft Word,** you also get to pick a Word template. I talk a little bit more about all this stuff in the Microsoft Word entry, so you may want to refer there.

World Wide Web The World Wide Web (also known as WWW or simply the Web) is a set of multimedia documents that are connected so you can jump from one document to another using **hyperlinks,** usually with just a click. The multimedia part means that you're not limited to words: you can place pictures, sounds, and even video clips in a Web document.

To view a WWW document, you need to have a **Web browser.** Popular Web browsers include Netscape Navigator, NCSA Mosaic, and Microsoft Internet Explorer. If you want to start exploring the Web, try using a search tool like Yahoo, which you can find at the **URL** address

http://www.yahoo.com.

It provides a directory of thousands of different World Wide Web sites.

ZIP I figured since this part of the book is called Outlook A to Z, I needed at least one "Z" entry. So let me tell you about ZIP. ZIP actually refers to a data-compression technique. When people say a **file** is ZIPped, they usually mean it's been compressed using the PKZIP or WINZIP utility. To use a ZIPped file, you have to unZIP it. If a file has been ZIPped with PKZIP, for example, you have to unZIP it with PKUNZIP.

ZIPping large files before you attach them to an e-mail message is a good idea—especially if you have the problems of limited disk space or slow transmission times. Ask your **administrator** for more information.

TROUBLE-SHOOTING

Got a problem? Starting on the next page are solutions to the problems that sometimes plague new users of Microsoft Outlook 97. You'll be on your way—and safely out of danger—in no time.

E-MAIL

You Don't Know Someone's E-Mail Address

You want to send so-and-so an e-mail **message**, but you don't have the address? Don't feel embarrassed. I think this is probably the most common e-mail problem of all. Really. Fortunately, this problem is easy to solve.

Check the Global Address List

If the certain someone to whom you want to send a message is an Outlook **user** on the same **network,** you can get the **e-mail name** from the **Global Address List.** To do this, click the Address Book button and follow these steps:

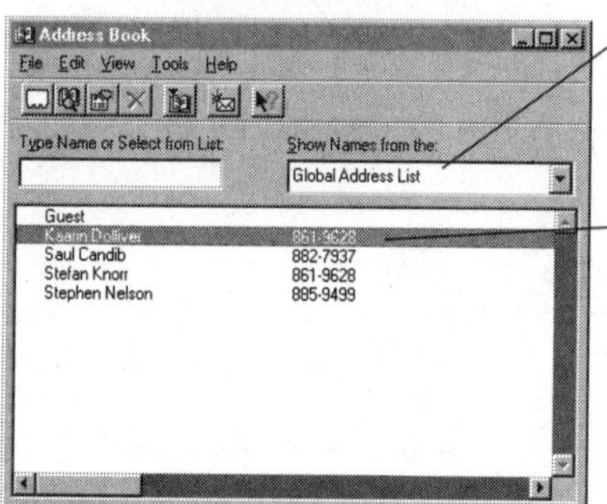

1 Select Global Address List from the Show Names From The list box.

2 Scroll through the list of names until you find the person to whom you want to send a message.

Call them and ask

If someone isn't a user on your network but your Outlook system is connected to the **Internet,** you can still send the message. You just can't look up the missing address in your Global Address List. Your best bet is to call and ask for the correct e-mail name. Sounds silly, doesn't it? But this really is the best solution. So go and

do it. You need to get both the person's e-mail name and the domain name. Once you know this information, you just send your message to

`e-mailname@domainname`

For example, if you wanted to send an e-mail message to me at my Microsoft Network address, you would send the message to:

`stphnlnlsn@msn.com`

stphnlnlsn is my Microsoft Network user name. And *msn.com* is the Microsoft Network domain name. If you're wondering where in the world I got my user name, it's just my first name, middle initial, and last name, without any vowels.

Ask them to e-mail you first

If you want to send someone e-mail but your real problem is that you're not familiar with this computerized, electronic mail thing, your best bet may be to get the other person to send you an e-mail message. (You may need to ask your **administrator** for your e-mail name and domain name if the other person will be sending you e-mail over the Internet.) But if you provide this information to the person with whom you want to correspond, and he or she is technically astute, it will be easy for the other person to send e-mail to you.

When you get the message—you'll see it in your **Inbox**—double-click it and read it. Then right-click the sender's name in the **message header** and choose the Add To Personal Address Book command when Outlook displays the shortcut menu. What you've just done is added the sender's e-mail name (and all the other information you need to send him or her e-mail messages) to your **Personal Address Book.**

continues

You Don't Know Someone's E-Mail Address *(continued)*

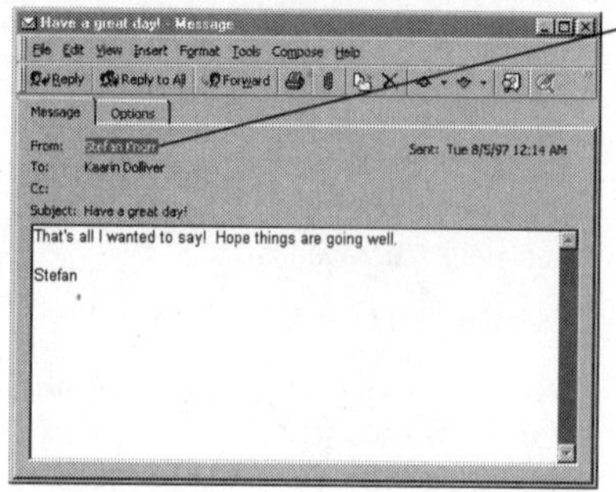

Right-click here to display the shortcut menu.

After you've added a person's name to your Personal Address Book, it's easy to address a message to the person. All you have to do is click the To or Cc button when you're writing the message so that Outlook displays the Select Names dialog box. Then follow these steps:

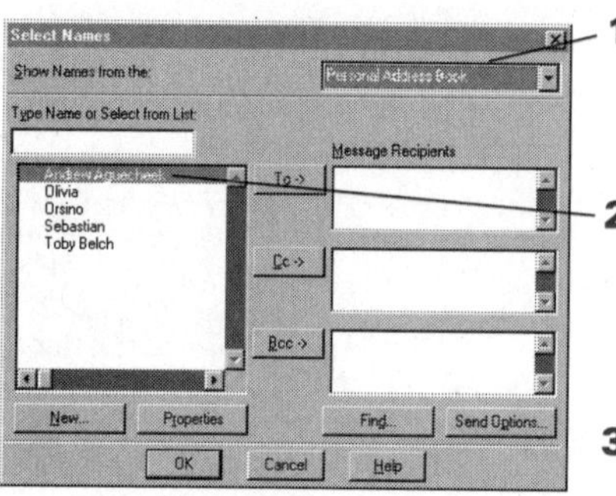

1. Select Personal Address Book from the Show Names From The list box.
2. Scroll through the list of names until you find the person to whom you want to send your message.
3. Double-click the person's name.

E-mail the user's postmaster

If for some reason you can't call the person or contact them some other way—maybe a quick letter—you can also try e-mailing a request to the postmaster at the e-mail post office that serves the host on which your friend is a user. I'm not really sure this will work, by the way. Sometimes it will, sometimes it won't. What you're really doing is asking for a special favor from the person who administers the e-mail messaging system for the domain. But to do this, you can usually e-mail your message to

```
postmaster@domainname
```

Of course, this means you need to know the domain name. So you may need to call the organization for that. But let's say that you want to e-mail a message to an old school chum. You know he works for Parnell Aerospace in Taiwan, but you don't know his user name. You need to call Parnell Aerospace and get the domain name of the Taiwan office—let's pretend it's parnell.com.tw. Then you e-mail your request to the following address:

```
postmaster@parnell.com.tw
```

Your Messages Aren't Getting Through

I don't have problems with my e-mail very often. And you probably won't either. Occasionally, however, your **messages** don't reach the **recipient.**

E-mail yourself a message to make sure Exchange Server is running

Your first step should be to e-mail yourself a message. You can do this simply by naming yourself in the message as the recipient. The **Outlook client** delivers the message to the Exchange server and then, assuming everything goes smoothly, the Exchange server delivers the message to your **Inbox.**

If you can't e-mail yourself a message, by the way, contact the **administrator.** The problem isn't actually yours to worry about: it's the administrator's problem. (Do, however, make sure you are really e-mailing yourself and not somebody else with a similar name in another department.)

continues

Your Messages Aren't Getting Through *(continued)*

Request a return receipt or a read notification receipt

If most of your messages reach their recipients but certain types don't seem to get through—or messages to certain recipients don't seem to get through—the problem might be one of human error. For example, Joe-Bob in purchasing might have forgotten that he received messages from you. In cases like these, you can tell Outlook to alert you to the fact that, for example, Joe-Bob has indeed received your message or that Joe-Bob has indeed read your message. To do this, click the Options tab when the **Message form** is displayed.

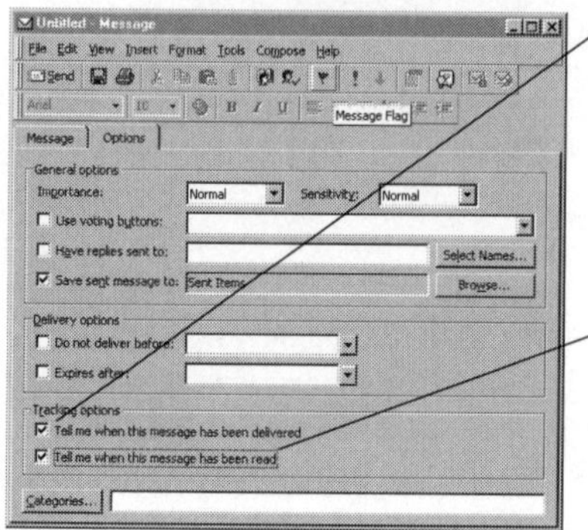

Check the Tell Me When This Message Has Been Delivered tracking option to have the server acknowledge delivery of your message.

Check the Tell Me When This Message Has Been Read tracking option to have the server monitor the recipient's Inbox and tell you when the recipient opened the message.

You're Getting Too Many Messages

In **organizations** where everybody uses e-mail, it's easy to get overwhelmed with e-mail **messages.** Secretaries. Managers with lots of direct and indirect subordinates. People in service departments. The truth is, short of an organizational e-mail policy that attempts to limit frivolous e-mail traffic, you can't do much to reduce the volume of incoming messages. But I do have three ideas for you if you're getting overloaded.

Don't use read receipts or delivery notifications wantonly

Okay, I know I said earlier that **read receipts** and **delivery receipts** are useful for dealing with the Joe-Bobs of the world. But they also clog up your **Inbox** with one or two extra messages for every message you send. So don't use them unless you have to.

Don't needlessly reply or forward messages

As sure as the sun rises in the east, the more messages you **reply** to and **forward,** the more you'll receive. The reason, of course, is that the recipient of a reply message or forwarded message generates another reply a certain percentage of the time. And this is true even if you shouldn't have created the reply message or forwarded the message in the first place.

I'm not suggesting that you stop replying to your boss's messages or that you not forward him or her messages when appropriate. But you should be judicious. It's easy to reply to or forward messages, but it isn't always necessary.

Use the Rules Wizard to filter messages

You can get Outlook's help when it comes to managing incoming messages. Just create a rule using the **Rules Wizard** that tells Outlook to reply, forward, or delete a message, as appropriate. To do this, choose Rules Wizard from the Tools menu and follow the Wizard's instructions. You can create rules describing the messages that Outlook can reply to, forward, or delete.

Are you getting junk mail?

If you're getting electronic mail from someone you'd rather not correspond with, you can use the **Rules Wizard** to automatically delete all messages you receive from that person. To do this, choose Rules Wizard from the Tools menu and follow the Wizard's instructions. Use the Wizard's dialog boxes to name the joker who keeps sending you e-mail and tell Outlook to delete any messages he sends you.

Your Folders Are Full

Folders can quickly overflow with messages if you regularly correspond via e-mail. Fortunately, it's easy to clean up a folder.

Delete individual messages you don't need

To delete a message, click it and then click the Delete button. If you want to save a copy of a message, be sure to print it before you delete it.

Empty a folder

You can delete all the messages in a folder by right-clicking the folder (to display the shortcut menu) and then choosing the Empty Folder command. It's a good idea to regularly remove the messages in the Deleted Items folder, for example. (When you delete a message in the **Inbox,** Outbox, or Sent Items folders, Outlook moves the message to the Deleted Items folder.)

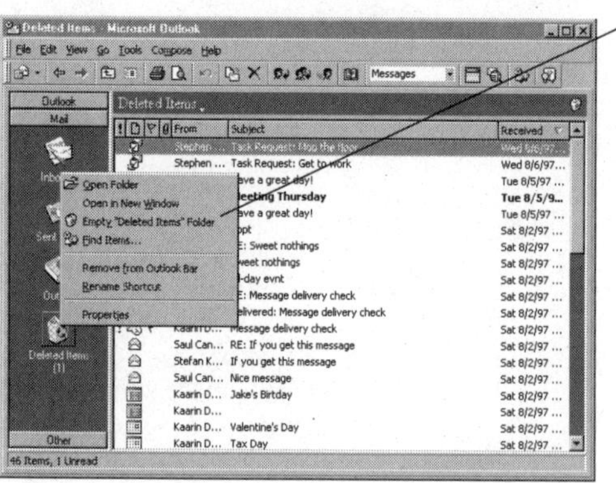

Choose the Empty "Deleted Items" Folder command to remove items from the selected folder.

CALENDAR AND TASKS

You Can't Schedule a Meeting

Outlook can be a marvelous tool for scheduling group meetings, but scheduling can be a challenge when people are busy. Nevertheless, there are some things you can do to make it easier to schedule meetings.

Use tentative appointments

Perhaps the easiest thing to do is tell Outlook that the **appointments** you schedule are **tentative appointments.** This way, the appointment time-slots you set aside don't fall into the **busy time** category, and Outlook can use them to schedule meetings. To indicate that an appointment is tentative, double-click the appointment to display the Appointment dialog box.

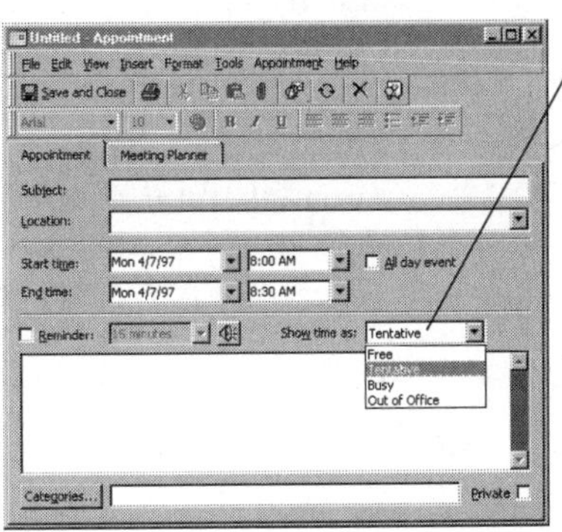

Click Tentative in the Show Time As box to designate the appointment as tentative.

Leave free time in your schedule

If you leave free time in your schedule—and everybody you work with does the same—you'll find it much easier to schedule meetings. You can even create a tentative appointment, perhaps called "meetings," and use it as an empty slot into which to plop real meetings. For real men and real women.

continues

You Can't Schedule a Meeting *(continued)*

Schedule shorter meetings

What Outlook looks for when it schedules a meeting is a chunk of free time that is available to every meeting attendee. For this reason, it's easier to schedule half-hour meetings than to schedule 1-hour meetings or 2-hour meetings. There are many more half-hour slots in a day than there are 1-hour or 2-hour slots, after all.

You Want Your Schedule and To Do List to Be Private

As you may know, almost everyone who uses Outlook can retrieve information from your **Calendar**. You may wonder, then, how private or public your schedule and **Task List** are. Unfortunately, I can't give you specific information about how private your schedule and Task list are, but I can give you some ideas for gaining a bit more privacy on the **network.**

Ask your administrator about delegate access permissions

You or the network **administrator** set what are called **delegate access permissions** to your schedule. Delegate access permissions determine who can view your Outlook information and whether they can change it. The default setting, by the way, is for other **users** to be able to view your Calendar and see when you're busy and when you're not. It's possible, however, for people to see much more detail. It all depends on the delegate access permissions.

One more thing: if people can view your daily or weekly calendar, they can see appointment and Task list descriptions as well. You can, however, use private text for appointment and task descriptions.

 **Private Appointments and Tasks**

Quick Reference

Any time you explore some exotic location, you're bound to see flora and fauna you can't identify. To make sure you can identify the commands and toolbar buttons you see in Microsoft Outlook 97, the Quick Reference describes these items in systematic detail.

Outlook Inbox Menu Commands

File Menu

New	Displays the New submenu of items you can create
	Mail Message Opens a new Message form
	Post In This Folder Displays the Post form so you can place a post message (or a file) in a folder
	Appointment Opens a new Appointment form
	Meeting Request Opens a new Meeting Request form
	Contact Opens a new Contact form
	Task Opens a new Task form
	Task Request Opens a new Task Request form
	Journal Entry Opens a new Journal Entry form
	Note Opens a new Note
	Office Document Opens a new Office document
	Choose Template Displays a list of templates you can use
	Choose Form... Opens a custom Outlook form
	Folder... Creates a new Folder in the information viewer
Open	Opens the selected folder so you can see its contents or the selected message so you can read it
Open Special Folder	Opens a Personal Folder or an Outlook Folder stored on the Exchange Server
Close All Items	Closes all open Outlook items, including items minimized to the Taskbar
Save As...	Saves the selected message in a different folder
Save Attachments	Saves any attachments to the selected message in a different folder

Folder	Displays the Folder submenu
	Create Subfolder... Creates a new subfolder in the selected folder
	Move... Moves the selected folder or message to a different location
	Copy... Copies the selected folder or message to a different location
	Copy Folder Design... Copies the design of the selected folder
	Delete Deletes the selected message or folder
	Rename... Renames the selected folder
	Add To Public Folder Favorites Adds the selected folder to the Favorites subfolder of Public Folders
	Remove From Public Folder Favorites Removes the selected folder from the Favorites subfolder of Public Folders
	Properties For Lets you view or change the Properties of the selected message or folder
Add To Outlook Bar...	Adds an icon for the selected folder or folders to the Outlook Bar
Import And Export...	Invokes the Import And Export Wizard
Archive...	Displays the Archive dialog box, enabling you to create Archive files
Page Setup	Displays the Page Setup submenu
	Table Style Opens the Page Setup: Table Style dialog box to let you set table style printing options for printing messages
	Memo Style Opens the Page Setup: Memo Style dialog box to let you set memo style printing options for printing messages
	Define Print Styles... Opens the Define Print Styles dialog box

continues

File Menu ***(continued)***

Print Preview	Displays a window that shows how printed messages look
Print...	Prints the selected message
Properties	Displays and lets you change the Properties of the selected item or folder
Exit	Stops the Microsoft Outlook client program
Exit And Log Off	Stops the Microsoft Outlook client program and any other workgroup programs

Edit Menu

Undo	Reverses, or undoes, the last action
Cut	Moves the current folder or item to the Clipboard
Copy	Moves a copy of the current folder or item to the Clipboard
Paste	Copies the Clipboard contents to the current folder
Clear	Deletes the selected item(s)
Select All	Selects all the messages in the open folder
Delete	Deletes the selected item(s)
Move To Folder...	Moves the selected item(s) to the folder you select
Copy To Folder...	Copies the selected item(s) to the folder you select
Mark As Read	Marks the selected message as one you've already read
Mark As Unread	Marks the selected message as one you haven't yet read
Mark All As Read	Marks all of the messages in the open folder as ones you've read
Categories...	Lets you assign the selected item(s) to a category

View Menu

Current View	Lets you change the current view of the information viewer
Show Fields...	Lets you add and remove fields (columns) to and from the current view
Format Columns...	Lets you specify what type of information appears in the columns of the information viewer
Sort...	Sorts messages using information that appears (or can appear) in the columns of the information viewer
Filter...	Lets you filter the messages in the information viewer so you only see those with specified characteristics
Group By...	Lets you group messages using information that appears (or can appear) in the columns of the information viewer
Expand/Collapse Groups	
	Collapse This Group Collapses a message group so the group shows but none of the messages do
	Expand This Group Uncollapses a message group so all of its messages show
	Collapse All Collapses all message groups so the groups show but none of the messages do
	Expand All Uncollapses all message groups so all of their messages show
Format View...	Lets you format all aspects of the current information viewer view
Define Views...	Lets you create new information viewer views and edit existing views
Field Chooser	Lets you define new fields and choose the fields available to include in views
Group By Box	Displays the Group By box, into which you can drag any column heading to group messages by that heading
AutoPreview	Displays a short preview of each message

continues

View Menu ***(continued)***

Toolbars	Displays the Toolbars submenu
	Standard Displays or hides the Standard toolbar
	Remote Displays or hides the Remote Mail toolbar
Status Bar	Displays or hides the Outlook program window's status bar (Outlook marks the command with a check mark when the status bar is present)
Folder List	Displays or hides the Folder List from the Outlook program window (Outlook marks the command with a check mark when the Folder List is present)
Outlook Bar	Displays or hides the Outlook Bar of items and folders

Go Menu

Back	Displays the previously selected folder
Forward	Displays the folder that was selected when Back was clicked
Up One Level	Displays the folder that contains the selected folder
Go To Folder...	Moves to a folder elsewhere on your hard drive or network
Inbox	Opens the Inbox folder
Calendar	Opens the Calendar folder
Contacts	Opens the Contacts folder
Tasks	Opens the Tasks folder
Journal	Opens the Journal folder
Notes	Opens the Notes folder
Sent Items	Opens the Sent Mail folder
Outbox	Opens the Outbox folder
Deleted Items	Opens the Deleted Items folder
My Computer	Opens My Computer

Tools Menu

Check For New Mail	Checks to see if new e-mail has arrived on the services you specify on the E-mail tab of the Tools menu Options dialog box
Check For New Mail On...	Lets you choose the services to check for new e-mail
Address Book...	Displays the Address Book
AutoSignature...	Displays the AutoSignature dialog box to let you create a signature for Outlook to append to each of your outgoing messages
Remote Mail	Displays the Remote Mail submenu
	Connect... Dials your computer from a remote location so you can download message headers
	Disconnect Ends the dial-up connection to your computer from a remote location
	Mark To Retrieve Marks the messages you wish to download to your computer when you reconnect
	Mark To Retrieve A Copy Marks the messages you wish to download to your computer while leaving a copy on the server
	Delete Removes messages both from your computer and from the server
	Unmark Cancels the status of a message that you had previously marked to download
	Unmark All Changes the status of all the messages that you had previously marked to download
	Remote Tools Displays the Remote toolbar

Tools Menu ***(continued)***

Synchronize	Displays the Synchronize submenu
	All Folders Updates all your offline folders so they match the server folders that Outlook uses for the actual delivery and storage of real messages
	This Folder Updates the selected offline folder so it matches its server folder
	Download Address Book Grabs the address lists from the Exchange Server's Address Book and stores them in the Address Book on your hard disk
Inbox Assistant	Starts the Rules Wizard, a tool for monitoring and managing incoming messages and other items
Out Of Office Assistant...	Starts the Out Of Office Assistant, a tool for monitoring and managing messages while you're out of your office or away from your computer
Dial	Displays the Dial submenu
	New Call... Let's you enter a new phone number or choose the phone number of a contact, and tells Outlook to dial the number for you
	Redial Lets you redial a phone number. You can pick from a menu of the last few numbers you dialed using Speed Dial
	Speed Dial Displays a menu of phone numbers you can dial with one click of the mouse
Record In Journal	Records the current item in the Journal
Find Items...	Locates messages that match your description
Find All	Displays the Find All submenu
	Related Messages... Finds all messages related to the current message
	Messages From Sender... Finds all messages sent by the sender of the current message
Empty "Deleted Items" Folder	Removes all the items from the Deleted Items folder

Services...	Describes and lets you change the information services available to the Outlook client
Options...	Displays a dialog box you can use to control how the Outlook client works

Compose Menu

New Mail Message	Displays the Message form so you can whip up a quick message
New Post In This Folder	Displays the Post form so you can place a post message (or a file) in a folder
Choose Template	Displays the Choose Template dialog box so you can create a new Outlook item using a template
Choose Form...	Displays the New Form dialog box so you can choose a custom form you want to use
Plan A Meeting...	Displays the Plan A Meeting dialog box so you can plan and schedule a meeting
Reply	Displays the RE: (reply) form so you can respond to a message by sending the sender a new message
Reply To All	Displays the RE: (reply) form so you can respond to a message by sending the sender and all of the other message recipients a new message
Post Reply In This Folder	Displays the New Post form so you can reply to a regular message or a post message by placing a new post message in a folder
Forward	Displays the FW: (forward) form so you forward a copy of a message to somebody else

Help Menu	
Microsoft Outlook Help	Displays the Office Assistant
Contents And Index	Displays the Microsoft Outlook Help Topics dialog box
What's This?	Adds a question mark to the pointer and displays an explanatory pop-up message the next time you click any item
Microsoft On The Web	Displays a submenu listing Web sites with useful information about Outlook
About Microsoft Outlook	Displays the About Microsoft Outlook dialog box and gives information about the available memory and system resources

OUTLOOK INBOX TOOLBAR TOOLS

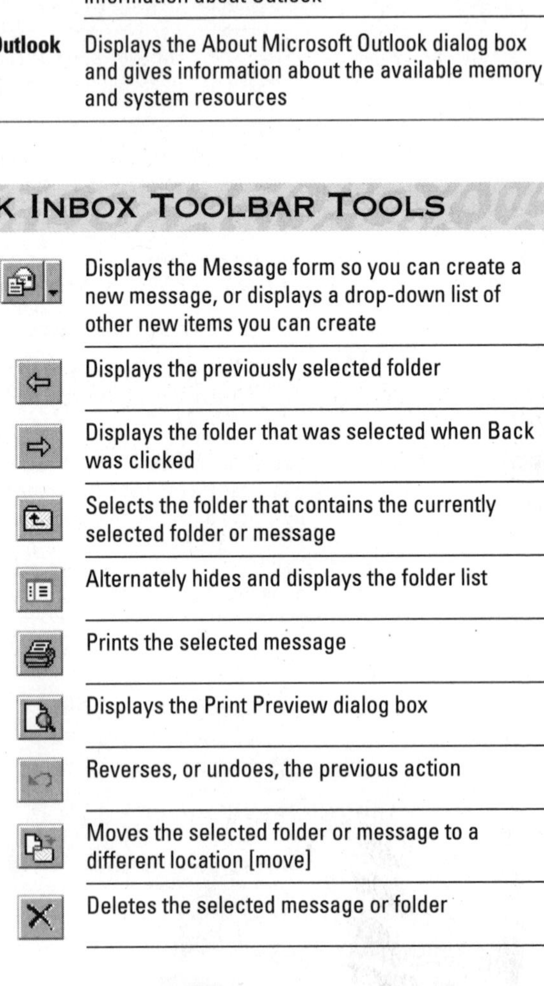

Displays the Message form so you can create a new message, or displays a drop-down list of other new items you can create

Displays the previously selected folder

Displays the folder that was selected when Back was clicked

Selects the folder that contains the currently selected folder or message

Alternately hides and displays the folder list

Prints the selected message

Displays the Print Preview dialog box

Reverses, or undoes, the previous action

Moves the selected folder or message to a different location [move]

Deletes the selected message or folder

 Displays the RE: (reply) form so you can respond to a message by sending the sender a new message

 Displays the RE: (reply to all) form so you can respond to a message by sending the sender and all of the other message recipients a new message

 Displays the FW: (forward) form so you forward a copy of a message to somebody else

 Displays the Address Book

By Sender — Displays a drop-down menu allowing you to select a View

 Toggles display of the Group By Box off and on

 Turns AutoPreview off and on

 Displays the Find dialog box to let you search for messages and other items

 Starts the Office Assistant Help guru

Inbox Message Form Commands

File Menu

New Displays a submenu of new items you can create

- **Mail Message** Opens a new Message form
- **Appointment** Opens a new Appointment form
- **Meeting Request** Opens a new Meeting Request form
- **Contact** Opens a new Contact form
- **Task** Opens a new Task form
- **Task Request** Opens a new Task Request form
- **Journal Entry** Opens a new Journal Entry form
- **Note** Opens a new Note

continues

File Menu—New *(continued)*

	Post In This Folder Displays the Post form so you can place a post message (or a file) in a folder
	Office Document Opens a new Office document
	Choose Template Displays a list of templates you can use
	Choose Form... Opens a custom Outlook form
Save	Saves the message in the selected folder
Save As...	Saves the message in the specified location
Save Attachments...	Displays a submenu of any attachments to the message
Publish Form As...	Displays the Publish Form As dialog box to let you distribute a new form on your network
Delete	Deletes the message
Move to Folder...	Moves the message to a different location
Copy to Folder...	Copies the message to a different location
Page Setup	Displays the Page Setup submenu
	Memo Style Opens the Page Setup: Memo Style dialog box to let you set memo style printing options for printing the message
	Define Print Styles... Opens the Define Print Styles dialog box
Print Preview	Displays a window that shows how the printed message will look
Print...	Prints the message
Properties	Displays and lets you change the Properties of the message
Send	Sends the message
Close	Closes the Message form window

Edit Menu

Command	Description
Undo	Reverses, or undoes, the last change to the message
Cut	Moves the current message selection to the Clipboard
Copy	Moves a copy of the current message selection to the Clipboard
Paste	Copies the Clipboard contents to the message
Paste Special...	Inserts the Clipboard contents or some portion of the Clipboard contents into the message
Clear	Deletes selected message text
Select All	Selects the entire message
Mark As Unread	Marks the message as unread in the information viewer
Message Flag...	Lets you add a "flag" to the message calling attention to an action you want the recipient to take in response
Categories...	Lets you assign the selected item(s) to a category
Find...	Looks for text that matches a specific description
Find Next	Looks for the next instance of text that matches a specific description
Links...	Describes, updates, and changes the selected object's links
Object	Displays a submenu of commands relating to the selected object
	Edit Opens the selected object so it can be modified
	Open Opens the application in which the selected object was created
	Properties Displays the Properties dialog box for the selected object

View Menu

Previous Displays the Previous submenu

Item Displays the previous message in the current folder

Unread Item Displays the previous unread message in the current folder

Item In Conversation Topic Displays the previous item in the current folder in the same conversation topic as the selected message

Item From Sender Displays the previous item in the folder from the same sender as the sender of the selected message

High Importance Item Displays the previous high importance item in the current folder

Flagged Message Displays the previous flagged message in the current folder

First Item In Folder Displays the first item in the current folder

Next Displays the Next submenu

Item Displays the next message in the current folder

Unread Item Displays the next unread message in the current folder

Item In Conversation Topic Displays the next item in the current folder in the same conversation topic as the selected message

Item From Sender Displays the next item in the folder from the same sender as the sender of the selected message

High Importance Item Displays the next high importance item in the current folder

Flagged Message Displays the next flagged message in the current folder

Last Item In Folder Displays the last item in the current folder

Message Header	Toggles between the full message header and the short message header
From Field	Displays or hides the From box in the Message form (Outlook marks the command with a check mark when the From box is present)
Bcc Field	Displays or hides the Bcc, or blind carbon copy, box in the Message form (Outlook marks the command with a check mark when the Bcc box is present)
Toolbars	Displays the Toolbars submenu
	Standard Displays or hides the Message form's standard toolbar (Outlook marks the command with a check mark when the toolbar is present)
	Formatting Displays or hides the Message form's formatting toolbar (Outlook marks the command with a check mark when the formatting toolbar is present)

Insert Menu

File...	Inserts a file into your message
Item...	Inserts a message (from one of your Outlook Folders) into your message
AutoSignature	Inserts your autosignature (if you have created one in the AutoSignature dialog box) into your message
Object...	Inserts an object into your message

Format Menu

Font...	Changes the font of the selected characters
Paragraph...	Changes the alignment of the selected paragraphs and adds or removes bullets

Tools Menu

Spelling...	Checks the spelling of the words you used in your message
AutoSignature...	Opens the AutoSignature dialog box to let you create a signature that you can automatically append to all your messages
Check Names	Verifies that you've correctly spelled the recipient names
Address Book	Displays the Address Book
Dial	Displays the Dial submenu
	New Call Let's you enter a new phone number or choose the phone number of a Contact, and tells Outlook to dial the number for you
	Redial Lets you redial a phone number you can pick from a menu of the last few numbers you dialed using Speed Dial
	Speed Dial Displays a menu of phone numbers you can dial with one click of the mouse
Record In Journal	Records the current item in the Journal
Find Items...	Locates messages that match your description
Find All	Displays the Find All submenu
	Related Messages... Finds all messages related to the current message
	Messages From Sender... Finds all messages sent by the sender of the current message
Recall This Message...	Attempts to retrieve a sent message before it is read by the recipient
Resend This Message...	Opens a copy of the message so you can send it again
Design Outlook Form	Opens the Message [Design] dialog box so you can design a custom form

Compose Menu

New Mail Message	Displays the Message form so you can whip up a quick message
New Post In This Folder	Displays the Discussion form so you can place a post message (or file) in a folder
Choose Template	Displays a list of templates you can use
Choose Form...	Displays the New Form dialog box so you can choose a custom form you want to use
Reply	Displays the RE: (reply) form so you can respond to a message by sending the sender a new message
Reply To All	Displays the RE: (reply) form so you can respond to a message by sending the sender and all of the other message recipients a new message
Post Reply In This Folder	Displays the Discussion form so you can reply to a regular message or a post message by placing a new post message in a folder
Forward	Displays the FW: (forward) form so you can forward a copy of a message to somebody else

Help Menu

Microsoft Outlook Help	Displays the Office Assistant
Contents And Index	Displays the Help Topics dialog box
What's This?	Adds a question mark to the pointer and displays an explanatory pop-up message the next time you click any item
Microsoft On The Web	Displays a submenu listing Web sites with useful information about Outlook
About Microsoft Outlook	Displays the About Microsoft Outlook dialog box and gives information about the available memory and system resources

MESSAGE FORM TOOLBAR BUTTONS

Send — Sends the message

Saves message in specified folder using specified name

Prints the message

Moves current selection to the Clipboard

Moves a copy of the current selection to the Clipboard

Copies the Clipboard contents to the Message form

Inserts a file into your message

Opens the Select Names dialog box

Checks recipient names

Lets you attach a message flag to the message

Sets the message importance to "high"

Sets the message importance to "low"

Toggles display of the message header on and off

Displays the Office Assistant

Seals your message with encryption

Lets you add a digital signature to your message

Interested in what the Formatting toolbar buttons do?

I'm not going to describe what the formatting tools do here. I already described them in the **Character Formatting** entry in this book.

Item-Specific Menu Commands

Calendar Menu

Command	Description
New Appointment	Lets you schedule a new appointment
New Event	Lets you schedule a new event
New Meeting Request	Lets you schedule a new invited event
Choose Template	Displays a list of templates you can use
Choose Form...	Displays the New Form dialog box so you can choose a custom form you want to use
New Recurring Appointment	Lets you schedule a new appointment that recurs regularly
New Recurring Event	Lets you schedule a new event that recurs regularly
New Recurring Meeting	Lets you schedule a new meeting that recurs regularly
Plan a Meeting...	Displays the Plan A Meeting dialog box so you can plan and schedule a meeting
Forward	Displays the FW: (forward) form so you can forward information about an appointment, meeting, or event to somebody else

Contacts Menu

Command	Description
New Contact	Lets you add a new contact to your Contact list
New Contact from Same Company	Lets you add to your Contact list a new contact from the same company as the selected contact
Choose Template	Displays a list of templates you can use
Choose Form...	Displays the New Form dialog box so you can choose a custom form you want to use
Explore Web Page	Takes you to the World Wide Web page of the selected contact
Plan A Meeting...	Displays the Plan A Meeting dialog box so you can plan and schedule a meeting
New Message To Contact	Lets you send a new message to someone on your Contact list

Contacts Menu *(continued)*

New Meeting With Contact	Lets you set up a meeting with someone on your Contact list
New Task For Contact	Assigns a new task to someone on your Contact list
New Letter to Contact	Starts the Microsoft Letter Wizard so you can send a new letter to someone on your Contact list
Forward	Lets you forward information about an appointment, meeting, or event to somebody else

Tasks Menu

New Task	Lets you add a new task to your Task List
New Task Request...	Lets you send a message requesting a task be performed
Choose Template	Displays a list of templates you can use
Choose Form...	Displays the New Form dialog box so you can choose a custom form you want to use
Forward	Lets you forward information about an appointment, meeting, or event to somebody else
Save Task Order	Saves the order of the current Task List

Journal Menu

New Journal Entry	Lets you add a new entry to your Journal
Choose Template	Displays a list of templates you can use
Choose Form...	Displays the New Form dialog box so you can choose a custom form you want to use
Forward	Lets you forward information about an appointment, meeting, or event to somebody else

Notes Menu

New Note	Lets you create a new note
Forward	Lets you forward information about an appointment, meeting, or event to somebody else

A

access permissions 48, 117, 162
actions 16
See also rules and actions; Rules Wizard
Address Book. *See also* Global Address List
adding e-mail names 16–17
adding to mail profile 44
and Contact list 44
defined 4, 16
distribution lists 51
using to send e-mail 19
Address Cards view 42, 43–44
addresses. *See* Global Address List; Personal Address Book
administrator 19, 48, 156–57, 162
alarms. *See* reminders
aliases, e-mail 52
aligning text 19
anniversaries, adding to Calendar 20, 34–35
announcements. *See* post messages
annual events
adding to Calendar 20, 34–35, 36
categorizing 35
keeping private 20
setting reminders 20
viewing list in Calendar 33
applications. *See* programs
appointments. *See also* events
adding to Calendar 21, 37
vs. events 55
private 117–19
recurring 122–23
rescheduling 48
setting reminders 125
shortcut for entering 37
tentative 144, 161
archives
creating 22–23
retrieving 24
attaching
attachments, defined 24
files to messages 87
files to post messages 113
Outlook items to e-mail messages 88
Outlook items to post messages 113–14
searching for attachments 61
AutoArchive feature 22–23
AutoAssistants
Inbox Assistant 25
Out Of Office Assistant 25
AutoDialer feature 25, 45
AutoPreview feature 26
AutoReply feature 27
AutoSignature feature 27–28

B

Bcc field 29
birthdays, adding to Calendar 20, 34–35
blind carbon copies 29
bullets, in e-mail messages 30
busy times, defined 31
buttons, toolbar, displaying names 39

C

Calendar
adding anniversaries 34–35
adding annual events 20, 34–35, 36
adding appointments 21
adding birthdays 34–35

calendar *(continued)*
- adding events 37, 56
- adding holidays 36
- Annual Events list 33
- busy times 31
- changing view 32–33, 47, 148
- column options 42
- Date Navigator 32, 33, 47–48
- delegate access
  - permissions 48, 117, 162
- displaying schedule 34, 37, 47
- display options 34, 47
- filtering items 60
- free time 31, 161
- overview 8–9, 31–32
- recurring appointments ... 122–23
- rescheduling appointments ... 48
- second time zone 130–31
- setting reminders 125
- shortcut for entering events 37
- troubleshooting 161–62
- Week view 32, 148

Calendar menu 79, 181
carbon copies 29, 46
Card view type 148
categories
- for annual events 35
- assigning 38
- filtering messages by 77
- for messages 38
- for notes 97
- searching by 61
- for tasks 38, 143

character formatting 39
Check Names feature 40
clients
- defined 40
- Outlook as client 40, 107
- vs. servers 133

coloring-coding notes 97, 98
columns. *See also* fields
- formatting 42
- Inbox display 41–42

company names, storing in
- Address Book 18

Compose menu (Inbox) 171
Compose menu (Message
- form) 179

composing
- e-mail messages 4–5, 86
- post messages 113

compound documents 101
Contacts folder
- adding names 43
- and Address Book 44
- Address Cards view 42, 43–44
- changing view 43
- dialing phone numbers 45
- finding items 60–62
- importing list from
  - Schedule+ 73–74
- looking up names 43–44
- overview 10–11, 42
- tracking contacts in
  - Journal 80–81

Contacts menu 181–82
conversation threads
- and e-mail messages 45
- and post messages 114

copying messages 29, 46
custom forms 46

D

data compression 152
Date Navigator 32, 33, 47–48
dates, selecting 47
Day view type 148
delegate access permissions 48, 117, 162
Deleted Items folder 84, 89, 160
delivery receipts 49, 158
designing forms 67

dialing telephone numbers
- from Address Book 18
- speed dialing 135–36
- using AutoDialer 25, 45

dialog boxes. *See* message boxes
digital signatures 50
directories. *See* folders
distribution lists
- creating 51
- overview 50
- using 51

domains, defined 52

E

Edit menu (Inbox) 166
Edit menu (Message form) 175
electronic mail. *See* e-mail
e-mail. *See also* distribution lists; messages, e-mail
- adding names to Address Book 16–17
- aliases 52
- confirming message delivery ... 49
- confirming message opening 121–22
- controlling amount 158–59
- defined 52
- deleting messages 160
- etiquette 53
- finding addresses 154–57
- forwarding messages 67, 90, 159
- problems with 157–58
- replying to messages 89–90, 126, 159
- troubleshooting 154–59

e-mail names 53
embedding
- existing OLE objects 53–54
- new OLE objects 55

emptying folders 160
encryption 55
etiquette
- flames 62–63

etiquette, e-mail 53
events
- adding to Calendar 37, 56
- vs. appointments 55
- defined 55
- recurring 20, 34–35, 36
- viewing information 56–57

Exchange server. *See* Microsoft Exchange server

F

Favorites folder 57, 103
fax numbers, storing in Address Book 18
Field Chooser 58
fields. *See also* columns
- adding to display 58
- changing display 58
- defined 57
- removing from display 58
- using Field Chooser 58

file extensions 59
File menu (Inbox) 164–66
File menu (Message form) ... 173–74
filenames 59
files
- attaching to messages 87
- compressing 152
- defined 59

filters
- in Calendar folder 60
- categorizing items 77
- in Inbox folder 75–77, 159
- overview 60
- in Task list 139

finding
- e-mail addresses 154–57
- Outlook items 60–62

flagging messages 92–93
flames 62–63
Folder Banner 64
folder list 64
folders. *See also* Calendar; Contacts folder; Inbox; Journal; notes; tasks
  Calendar
  Calendar folder 31–37
  Contacts
  creating 63
  creating views 65, 150
  defined 63
  deleting messages 160
  displaying list 64
  emptying 160
  Favorites folder 57, 103
  filtering items 60
  folders within 138
  Inbox
  information viewer 78
  My Computer folder 103
  My Documents folder 103
  naming 63
  offline 100, 126
  other 102–4
  in Outlook 6–7
  overview 102
  personal 112
  private 119
  public 104, 120
  switching views 106, 150
  synchronizing 139
  troubleshooting 160
  using views 65
  viewing hierarchy 64
fonts 66
Format menu (Message form) 177
formatting
  e-mail messages 39
  folder columns 42
forms. *See also* Message form
  custom 46
  defined 66
  designing 67
forwarding
  e-mail messages 67, 90, 159
  post messages 116
free time 31, 161

G

Global Address List 51, 68, 154
  See also Address Book
Go menu (Inbox) 168
grouping
  e-mail messages 45, 68–70
  post messages 114
  tasks 68–69
groups, expanding and collapsing 70

H

Help feature 70
  See also Office Assistant
Help menu (Inbox) 172
Help menu (Message form) 179
holidays, adding to Calendar 36
HTML 71
hyperlinks 71–72

I

icons, toolbar, displaying names 39
Icon view type 148
importance, message 72
Import And Export Wizard ... 73–74
importing contacts from Schedule+ 73–74

Inbox
- column options 41–42
- defined 6–7
- deleting messages 160
- emptying 160
- menus 79, 164–72
- overview 74
- previewing messages 26
- read vs. unread messages 120
- received messages 89
- toolbar buttons 172–73
- using filters 75–77, 159
- view options 148–49

Inbox Assistant 75, 126
- *See also* Rules Wizard

information services 77
Information Store 78
information viewer 78
Insert menu (Message form) ... 177
international date line 130
Internet
- defined 78–79
- World Wide Web 152

items. *See also* appointments; Contacts folder; Journal; meetings; messages, e-mail; notes; tasks
- defined 79
- item-specific menus ... 79, 181–82
- sorting 134–35

J

Journal
- automatic recordkeeping ... 80–82
- manual recordkeeping 83
- menus 79, 182
- overview 12–13, 80
- tracking activities 80–82
- uses for 80–81

Journal menu 79, 182
junk mail 159

L

LANs 40
linking, OLE objects 53–54
local area networks (LANs) 40

M

mail. *See* messages, e-mail
Mailbox 84
- *See also* Inbox

Mail folders 84
marking e-mail messages 120
Meeting Planner. *See* meetings
meetings
- adding to schedule 37
- keeping short 162
- and permissions 48, 117, 162
- scheduling 84–85, 162
- shortcut for entering 37

megabytes, defined 85
menus, item-specific 79, 181–82
message boxes 92
message flag 92–93
Message form
- adding hyperlinks 71–72
- aligning text in 19
- bullets in messages 30
- creating OLE objects 53–55
- finding text 62
- formatting messages 39
- menu commands 173–79
- message body 91
- message header 94
- overview 4–5, 93–94
- sensitivity level 132–33
- toolbar buttons 180
- using fonts 66
- writing messages 4–5, 86

messages, e-mail. *See also* Message form
- adding hyperlinks 71–72
- assigning priority 72
- attaching files 87
- attaching OLE objects 88
- attaching Outlook items 88
- automatic delivery 26
- automatic replies 27
- bullets in 30
- composing 4–5, 86
- confirming delivery 49
- confirming opening 121–22
- conversation threads 45
- defined 86
- delegate access permissions ... 48, 117, 162
- deleting 89, 160
- filtering 75–77, 159
- finding 60–62
- finding text in 62
- flagging 92–93
- flames 62–63
- forwarding 67, 90, 159
- grouping 45, 68–70
- identifying subject 138
- incoming 6–7
- marking 120
- message body 91
- message header 94
- and Out Of Office Assistant 108–10
- previewing 26
- printing 91
- reading 6–7, 89
- read vs. unread 120
- receiving 6–7
- replying to ... 27, 89–90, 126, 159
- sealing 50, 130
- sending 4–5, 88
- sending copies 29, 46
- sensitivity level 132–33
- setting options 94–95

messages *(continued)*
- signatures 27–28
- sorting 134–35
- spell checking 136–37
- ungrouping 68–69

Microsoft Exchange server
- checking status of 157
- defined 2, 40, 107
- delivery receipts 49, 158
- information services 77
- read receipts 121–22, 158

Microsoft Word, as e-mail editor 95–96

MIME 96

monthly calendar. *See* Date Navigator

Month view type 148

moving notes 98

My Computer folder 103

My Documents folder 103

N

names
- adding to Address Book ... 16–17
- e-mail names 53
- finding addresses 154–57
- in Global Address List 51, 68, 154
- in Personal Address Book 155–56
- verifying using Check Names 40

netiquette 53

network administrator 19, 48, 156–57, 162

networks. *See also* Internet; Microsoft Exchange server
- defined 97
- LANs 40
- and Outlook 2–3

notes
- categorizing ... 97
- coloring ... 97, 98
- customizing ... 97–98
- deleting ... 98
- keeping track of ... 98
- moving ... 98
- overview ... 12–13, 97
- resizing ... 98
- writing ... 97

Notes menu ... 79, 182
numbers. *See* phone numbers

O

objects. *See* OLE objects
Office Assistant ... 99–100
offline folders ... 100, 126, 139
OLE, defined ... 101
OLE objects
- attaching to messages ... 88
- in e-mail messages ... 53–55
- existing, embedding ... 53–54
- existing, linking ... 53–54
- linked vs. embedded ... 101
- new, embedding ... 55

online Help ... 70
online services ... 102
organization, defined ... 102
Outbox folder ... 84
Outlook
- importing Schedule+ contacts ... 73–74
- navigating ... 104–5
- overview ... 2–3

Outlook Bar
- accessing folders ... 105–6
- changing folder views ... 106
- customizing ... 106
- navigating Outlook ... 104–5
- overview ... 104
- when to use ... 107

Outlook client ... 2, 40, 107
Outlook folders ... 107
- *See also* folders

Out Of Office Assistant
- AutoReply feature ... 27
- creating standard response ... 108
- defined ... 25, 108
- list of actions ... 110
- rules and actions ... 108–9, 126
- using ... 110

P

passwords ... 111
permissions ... 111
- *See also* delegate access permissions

Personal Address Book. *See also* Address Book
- adding names ... 16–17, 155–56
- adding to mail profile ... 44
- and Contact list ... 44
- distribution lists ... 51
- overview ... 4, 112
- using to send e-mail ... 19

personal folders ... 112
phone numbers
- dialing ... 18, 25, 45
- speed dialing ... 135–36
- storing in Address Book ... 18
- tracking calls ... 82

Plan A Meeting dialog box ... 85
pop-up boxes ... 112
posting post messages ... 114
post messages
- attaching files ... 113
- attaching Outlook items ... 113–14
- and conversation threads ... 114
- forwarding ... 116
- grouping ... 114
- overview ... 112

post messages *(continued)*
- posting 114
- printing 116
- public folders for 113, 120
- reading 114
- replying to 115
- writing 113

previewing incoming messages 26
printing
- messages 91
- post messages 116

prioritizing tasks 143
priority level, e-mail 72
privacy
- delegate access permissions ... 48, 117, 162
- keeping appointments private 21, 117–19
- keeping recurring events private 20
- maintaining 162

private appointments 117–19
private folders 119
private tasks 117–19
programs, defined 119
program windows, defined 119
project management 38, 143
protocols
- MIME 96
- SMTP 134

public folders 104, 112, 113, 120

R

reading
- e-mail messages 89
- post messages 114

read receipts 121–22, 158
receipts
- delivery receipts 49, 158
- read receipts 121–22, 158

recordkeeping. *See* Journal
recurring appointments 122–23
recurring events
- adding to Calendar 20, 34–35, 36
- appointments 122–23
- categorizing 35
- keeping private 20
- setting reminders 20
- viewing list 33

recurring tasks 123–24
registered mail. *See* delivery receipts; read receipts
reminders 20, 125
Remote Mail feature 125–26
replying
- to e-mail messages 27, 89–90, 126, 159
- to post messages 115

rescheduling appointments 48
resizing notes 98
Rolodex. *See* Address Book; Address Cards view
rules and actions
- applying rules 129
- customizing rules 129
- defined 126
- using Rules Wizard 127–29

Rules Wizard 127–29

S

Schedule+
- and Calendar 31
- importing contacts to Outlook 73–74
- overview 130

scheduling. *See also* Calendar
- and access permissions 48, 117, 162
- displaying schedule 47
- free time 31, 161
- meetings 84–85, 162

sealed messages 50, 130
second time zone 130–31
security. *See also* privacy
  digital signatures 50
  encryption 55
  overview 132
sending e-mail
  automatic delivery 26
  overview 4–5, 88
  sender, defined 132
sensitivity, message 132–33
Sent Items folder 84
servers 2, 40, 133
  See also Microsoft Exchange server
signatures
  creating 28
  digital signatures 50
  for e-mail 27–28
smileys 134
SMTP (simple mail transport protocol) 134
sorting 134–35
Speed Dial feature 135–36
spelling checker 136–37
Start menu 62
status bar 138
street addresses, storing in Address Book 18
subfolders 138
subjects, in message header 138
synchronizing folders 139

T

Table view type 148
TaskPad 9, 140
tasks
  accepting 142
  adding to Task list 140–41
  assigning to others 141–42
  categorizing 38, 143
  declining 142
  defined 140
  filtering 139
  finding 60–62
  grouping 38, 68–69
  prioritizing 143
  private 117–19
  reassigning 142
  recurring 123–24
  reporting status 144
  setting reminders 125
  tracking status 143
  ungrouping 68–69
  viewing Task list 141
Tasks menu 79, 182
telephone numbers
  dialing 18, 25, 45
  speed dialing 135–36
  storing in Address Book 18
tracking calls 82
tentative appointments 144, 161
text
  aligning 19
  filtering messages by 76
  finding in messages 62
threads. *See* conversation threads
Timeline view type 148
time zone, second 130–31
To Do list. *See* tasks
toolbars
  displaying button names 39
  Inbox tools 172–73
  Message form 180
  overview 145
Tools menu (Inbox) 169–71
Tools menu (Message form) 178
ToolTips 39
tracking. *See* Journal
troubleshooting
  Calendar 161–62
  e-mail 154–59
  folder use 160

U

undoing actions 145
ungrouping
  messages 68–69
  tasks 68–69
unread messages 120
URLs 146
users, defined 146
Uuencode 146–47

V

View menu (Inbox) 167–68
View menu (Message
    form) 176–77
views
  Calendar 32–33, 47, 148
  creating 65, 150
  Inbox 148–49
  modifying 149
  switching 106, 150
  types of 147–48

W

Web browsers 151
Web pages 151
Week view type 32, 148
wizards
  Import And Export
    Wizard 73–74
  Rules Wizard 127–29
Word. *See* Microsoft Word
WordMail 96, 151
World Wide Web 152
writing
  e-mail messages 4–5, 86
  post messages 113

Z

ZIP files 152

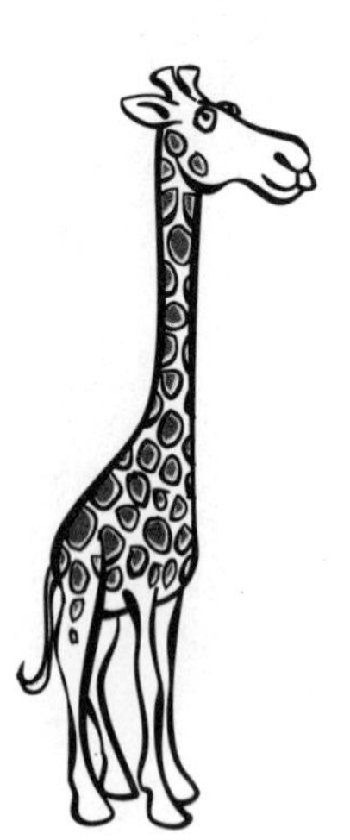

The manuscript for this book was prepared and submitted to Microsoft Press in electronic form. Text files were prepared using Microsoft Word 7.0 for Windows. Pages were composed by Stephen L. Nelson, Inc., using PageMaker 6.0 for Windows, with text in Minion and display type in Copperplate. Composed pages were delivered to the printer as electronic prepress files.

COVER DESIGNER
Gregory Erickson

COVER ILLUSTRATOR
Eldon Doty

INTERIOR TEXT DESIGNER
The Understanding Business

PAGE LAYOUT
Stefan Knorr

COPY EDITOR
Paula Thurman

WRITERS
Stephen Nelson & Saul Candib

TECHNICAL EDITOR
Kaarin Dolliver

INDEXER
Julie Kawabata

Printed on recycled paper stock.